Praise for
Dr. Paul White and *The Vibrant Workplace*

Sadly, we still need this book. Fifty-one percent of managers believe they are doing a good job of recognizing good work. Only 17 percent of their employees agree. That statistic from *The Vibrant Workplace* shows why we need Paul White's splendid new book. He explains why our typical ways of showing appreciation—like recognition programs—rarely live up to the hype. But he doesn't leave us hanging. He tells us how we can show appreciation in ways that actually matter to others at work. Consider buying two copies, one for yourself and one for your boss.

RICK MAURER
Author, *Beyond the Wall of Resistance*

Misconceptions abound on what is needed to create a healthy, thriving, and engaged workforce. In *The Vibrant Workplace*, Dr. White shatters these misconceptions with research-based insight into how employees are motivated. Not stopping there, *The Vibrant Workplace* also provides practical steps on how to overcome the most common obstacles to employee engagement.

JACK W. BRUCE
Past President of SHRM-Atlanta

The Vibrant Workplace dispels the myth that employee engagement is a simple program you just purchase and require management to deliver. In this book, Dr. White furnishes best practices and practical tools to create a path to a healthy organization. He provides a deeper understanding on ways to connect with and empower your team to grow and create caring relationships.

EVAN WILSON
Chief Experience Officer
Meritrust Credit Union

The Vibrant Workplace is written just like we need it: practical, topical, and experiential. As a coach, understanding the obstacles to advancing a vibrant workplace culture is key to helping clients and their organizations. Dr. White delivers insights into dealing with a variety of distinct situations, environments, and attitudes. Readers are given what is needed to create specific, actionable steps and build their own vibrant workplace. *The Vibrant Workplace* is like having a coach-in-a-book!

DAN AGNE
Owner and Principal Consultant
The Agne Group, LLC

I frequently recommend *The 5 Languages of Appreciation in the Workplace* by Gary Chapman and Paul White in seminars and workshops I teach because it's an "aha" for many people. Paul White's latest book, *The Vibrant Workplace*, is an invaluable companion to *5 Languages* because it identifies the common obstacles to increasing appreciation in the workplace and shows you how to address them. Now I'll be recommending both books.

MICHAEL LEE STALLARD
Speaker, workshop leader, and author of *Fired Up or Burned Out* and *Connection Culture*

Over the past ten years I've had a chance to work with several companies, and it would be extremely rare to find a company, or even a department, that could be described as "vibrant"—full of energy and enthusiasm. The good news is that in this book, Dr. Paul White shares with us a practical approach on how we *can* create vibrant workplaces through the languages of appreciation.

DANA MCARTHUR
Founder, McArthur Creative

The Vibrant Workplace covers all the bases. Whether it's an organization that has no structured appreciation or recognition program in place, or an organization with a flourishing appreciation culture, Dr. White offers practical insights and ideas for meeting the needs of today's workforce to feel appreciated and valued for the contributions they make every day.

LISA HOLLEY
Corporate Learning and Development Consultant
Insperity, Inc.

If you want to revitalize your organization and enhance employee engagement, this book is a great resource. In *The Vibrant Workplace*, Dr. White provides tips and tools on how to overcome the practical challenges of implementing and sustaining a culture of appreciation in the workplace—by using personalized and effective ways of communicating authentic appreciation at work.

JASMINE LIEW
Organization Development Director, Breakthrough Catalyst
Singapore

When we talk about workplaces, the typical adjectives are: task-oriented, stressful, high pressure. Yet I was delighted to read *The Vibrant Workplace*, which gives us an alternative—that our workplace can be people-centric, vibrant, and engaging! Sharing solid research and his personal experience, Dr. White gives many practical tips and suggestions to build such a culture via personalized and culture-sensitive appreciation.

ANDREW MA
Chorev Consulting International Ltd.
Hong Kong

THE
VIBRANT
WORKPLACE

Overcoming the Obstacles to
Building a Culture of Appreciation

DR. PAUL WHITE

NORTHFIELD PUBLISHING
CHICAGO

Edited by Elizabeth Cody Newenhuyse
Interior design: Ragont Design
Cover design: Erik M. Peterson
Author photo: Michael Bankston

Library of Congress Cataloging-in-Publication Data

Names: White, Paul E., 1957- author.
Title: The vibrant workplace : overcoming the obstacles to creating a culture
  of appreciation / Paul E. White ; foreword by Gary Dr. Chapman.
Description: Chicago : Northfield Publishing, 2017.
Identifiers: LCCN 2016059712 (print) | LCCN 2017001945 (ebook) | ISBN
  9780802415035 (paperback) | ISBN 9780802495174
Subjects: LCSH: Leadership. | Employee motivation. | Personnel management. |
  BISAC: BUSINESS & ECONOMICS / Leadership. | BUSINESS &
ECONOMICS /
  Management.
Classification: LCC HD57.7 .W4585 2017 (print) | LCC HD57.7 (ebook) |
DDC
  658.3/14--dc23
LC record available at https://lccn.loc.gov/2016059712

We hope you enjoy this book from Northfield Publishing. Our goal is to provide high-quality, thought-provoking books and products that help you in all your relationships. For more information, go to northfieldpublishing.com or write to:

Northfield Publishing
820 N. La Salle Boulevard
Chicago, IL 60610

1 3 5 7 9 10 8 6 4 2

Printed in the United States of America

CONTENTS

FOREWORD

When Dr. Paul White and I wrote the original book, *The 5 Languages of Appreciation in the Workplace,* we knew that it had the potential of greatly enhancing the emotional climate in the workplace. We knew this because we had spent two years doing pilot projects in all types of businesses: from beauty salons to construction companies. We saw "job satisfaction" scores increase dramatically. We also knew that when people feel appreciated they are far more engaged in their work, and thus more productive.

In the past five years, Dr. White has been involved in teaching and training many organizational leaders how to be more successful in their efforts to express appreciation. Many did not know the difference between "recognition" and "appreciation." Many genuinely thought they were expressing appreciation—but the majority of their employees did not feel appreciated. Those who were open to using the Motivating by Appreciation Inventory to discover each person's primary "appreciation language" found tremendous buy-in from their employees. These men and women openly expressed how their level of motivation and commitment to the company were greatly enhanced.

However, in seeking to help companies implement this personalized approach to expressing appreciation, Dr. White discovered some common obstacles to gaining the full potential of the power of effective appreciation. The purpose of this new volume, *The Vibrant Workplace,* is to identify those obstacles and give practical help in how to overcome these barriers and create a culture of appreciation. The benefits received are well worth the effort.

For those of you who have read *The 5 Languages of Appreciation in the Workplace,* this sequel will be extremely helpful in navigating the waters of positive change. For those who have not read the original book, this book will prove highly beneficial, because *The Vibrant Workplace* will give you advanced information on how to avoid or overcome some of the typical barriers to success. However, to gain maximum return on your investment of time, I strongly recommend reading both books.

Learning to implement these tried and proven ways of expressing appreciation will create a more positive work environment. This in turn leads to greater engagement and productivity among employees. The power of effective appreciation cannot be overestimated.

GARY D. CHAPMAN, PHD
Author of *The 5 Love Languages*®:
The Secret to Love That Lasts

INTRODUCTION

*"Vibrant": full of energy and enthusiasm.
Spirited, lively, energetic, full of life.*

"Vibrant"? Can a workplace be vibrant? Busy, yes. Sometimes fun. But "vibrant"? Really?

That's exactly the point: it's something we all long for, if we think about it. The vibrant workplace connotes energy, positivity, and growth—characteristics we desire for the environment where we spend the majority of our waking hours. A vibrant workplace draws people to it—quality, talented employees want to work in a healthy context and become a part of the life-exuding process. Employees bring their own gifts and unique personalities to add to the synergy in a dynamic work setting. A vibrant workplace is the antithesis of how many work environments are described: negative, energy-sapping, and toxic to growth.

A vibrant workplace is the result of an organization that has a clear purpose and mission, is rooted in the resources necessary to grow, and whose individual members work together to grow the organization and produce quality goods and services.

But, to be clear, a vibrant workplace isn't a perfect, utopian organization that is without struggles or challenges. In fact, the vibrant workplace actually can exist in the same external conditions as a toxic workplace. But somehow, this particular culture has found ways to

9

resist and repel negative influences, to train team members to build healthy internal processes, and to continually put forth positive energy toward the organization's goals.

How does all this happen?

THE DRIVING FORCE

A healthy organization can't develop without authentic appreciation—a core component and driving force for a vibrant workplace to grow and prosper. Why is this so important? Because authentic appreciation:

- affirms the value of each member of the organization, helping them function better and grow in their competencies;
- communicates directly at a personal level between team members, rather than the indirect impersonal messages typically sent in an unhealthy workplace;
- creates proactive energy for the recipient, for the sender, for others observing, and for the organization as a whole;
- serves as a "repellent" and protector against negative influences that can damage the members of the community;
- displays genuine affirmation—not faked displays or a cheap imitation, and not just trying to look like the real thing;
- gives team members the energy and stamina to overcome the obstacles encountered in everyday work life.

BREAKING DOWN THE BARRIERS

As I have worked with thousands of employees, supervisors, managers, and HR professionals across the world, the need for a resource to help leaders and organizations successfully create a vibrant, energetic work environment became clear. The negativity, pessimism, and toxic workplaces encountered were initially almost overwhelming. But we found that assisting leaders in successfully implementing authentic appreciation within their organization was the key to pursuing a vibrant workplace.

While many managers and HR directors are excited about learning how to create a more positive work environment with the 5 languages of appreciation, they also encounter common challenges in trying to do so. As I tell groups when I am speaking, "Behavior change is difficult—both individually and collectively. Otherwise, we would all be svelte, in good physical shape, and be able to achieve all the goals we have set for ourselves. Change requires overcoming obstacles; so to be successful you have to identify the potential barriers and ways to overcome them."

Whether you are a CEO, HR director, department manager, or an employee struggling with difficult workmates, this book is for you. We will look at the obstacles employers and employees most commonly face as they seek to successfully implement the concept of authentic appreciation in the workplace. We will identify the challenges and explore where they come from. Then we will look at the ways to get past the obstacles. Sometimes we break down the obstacles and go *through* them, while other times we may figure out a way *around* them, or we may learn how to climb *over* them!

I get questions like these all the time from managers and employees:

"My supervisor is all about results—getting tasks done and showing profitability. What can I do if he really isn't that interested in appreciation and doesn't see the need for it?"

"Our workplace is so negative and jaundiced. They feel the employee recognition program is a joke. No one trusts management anymore. Can anything be done to get us past all this?"

"I see the need to encourage and support our staff but everyone is already overloaded. I don't see how we would have time

11

to communicate appreciation to one another—we barely have the time to say 'hi' in between seeing patients and getting all of the paperwork done. Is communicating appreciation to others really realistic?"

I have organized the chapters and topics around these and other frequently asked questions. My hope is that this book will be accessible and relatable to a wide variety of settings and needs.

WHAT WE WANT THIS BOOK TO DO FOR YOU

The goals of this book are to:

1) Equip employers with the foundational tools necessary to create a vibrant workplace through authentic appreciation;
2) Identify, clarify, and describe the most common obstacles to applying the 5 languages of appreciation in the workplace;
3) Provide a deeper understanding of the issues and dynamics that underlie the obstacles; and
4) Give practical action steps and resources that individuals can take to successfully implement authentic appreciation in spite of the barriers encountered.

The goal of the book is *not* to rehash, review, or replace the content presented in *The 5 Languages of Appreciation in the Workplace*. If you have not yet read this bestselling foundational explanation of the importance of appreciation in the workplace, what the 5 languages of appreciation look like in daily life, and the role of our online assessment, the Motivating by Appreciation Inventory, then it would be wise to purchase that as a companion volume.

Nor will this book replace the information, resources, and training provided through our online resources. If you would like to explore these further, go to www.appreciationatwork.com.

HOW TO USE THIS BOOK

This book is organized around the questions asked by real people in real workplaces. Therefore, you do not need to read the book front to back. Rather, you can pick the chapters that address the challenges of most concern to you.

The chapters are arranged in a sequence of the most frequently voiced concerns, as well as those issues that are most foundational. For example, if you are not able to address and solve the problem of a lack of support from your supervisor or management, the other issues are largely a moot point.

Feel free to pick and choose, finding the parts of the book that are most relevant to you currently, and learn how to overcome those obstacles. Then move on to other areas of interest or challenge.

Please note that I have chosen to write the chapters utilizing a variety of formats, for two primary reasons. First, the content and issues addressed in some chapters are better covered in different formats (such as a Q&A format in "Unique Settings"). Second, I believe the variety and change of pace of presentation and style of thinking make for a more interesting, engaging read. (I hope you agree!)

Given that the issues addressed in each chapter come from the real world of work and from those who are actively pursuing authentic appreciation in their workplace, I believe you will find the information relevant and practically useful in your workplace as well.

"THE SILENCE IS DEAFENING"

Employees in every type of workplace are discouraged. Their position within the organization doesn't matter. They can be frontline workers, supervisors, department heads, midlevel managers within large organizations—even executives and business owners.

And the dejection runs across all types of work settings: small businesses, schools, medical settings, large manufacturing firms, government agencies, universities, long-term care facilities. *Where* you work really doesn't matter. The negativity seems to be everywhere.

Why is there such a theme of despair in most workplaces? Because people want to be appreciated for what they do at work. But, unfortunately, most people *don't* feel appreciated at work.

©Glasbergen
glasbergen.com

GLASBERGEN

"Every time you do something right, I will punch your rewards card. When you reach 10,000 punches, you earn a high five."

Most of us don't want to just put in the time and collect our paycheck. We want to use our skills, education, experience—who we are—to make a difference. Not only do we want to make valuable contributions to our employer and clients, but we would like *others* to notice and value us, as well.

Andy, an accountant friend of mine, told me: "I give my best efforts at work. I try to be thorough and do things correctly. I get my work done on time, and I'm willing to work late to complete last minute requests by my boss. But I never hear *anything*; in fact, the silence is deafening. Well, that's not exactly right. If I make a mistake or am a little late on something, she jumps all over me. I'm not sure how much longer I can take it." (In fact, he left to take a position at another company within six months.)

Numerous studies over the years have repeatedly found this to be the case, and we provide a thorough review of the research in *The 5 Languages of Appreciation in the Workplace*. However, let me cite one representative example from a national study across numerous corporations:

While 51 percent of managers surveyed across several companies felt they were doing a good job of recognizing employees for work well done, only 17 percent of the employees who worked for those managers felt appreciated by their supervisor.[1] Thus, there was a wide discrepancy between how the managers felt they were doing in providing recognition, and what their employees experienced.

This pattern contrasts with what employees report they desperately desire:

Over 200,000 global employees were studied by the Boston Consulting Group, and the top reason they reported enjoying their work was "feeling appreciated" (#2 was having a good relationship with their supervisor, and #4 was that they had a good relationship with their colleagues. Financial compensation didn't appear until #8).[2]

Four out of five employees (81%) say they are motivated to work harder when their boss shows appreciation for their work.[3] You have probably heard the stories of employees who received a handwritten note or an email from their boss that they filed and kept for years. What did the note say? Their employer or supervisor thanked them for the work they did, or for some small way they helped a customer. Why did they save it? Because to them it was *golden*—rare and valuable.

THE COST TO ORGANIZATIONS

When staff don't feel valued, bad things happen—to the individual employee, to the work group, and to the organization.

"I'm sick of this," Thomas said. "I work hard, stay late, answer emails from home—and it's never enough. They always want more—more *of* me, and more *from* me. Yet I never hear anything positive. Why should I continue to 'kill myself' to do what they want, when it doesn't seem to matter? I'm done. I'll go in and put in my time but no more."

"Employee engagement" has become a hot term in the world of work and a focus of much research. Why? Because researchers have found that when an employee is actively engaged in their work and workplace, positive results follow for the organization: increased productivity, lower staff turnover, less absenteeism, fewer on-site accidents, more attention to procedures and policies. On the other hand, the disengaged employee is physically present, but mentally and emotionally they've checked out. Not what you want in your workers!

A natural result of not feeling appreciated is to not work as hard. Why put forth the effort when no one seems to care? Other negative outcomes become evident when staff don't feel valued:

- Increased tardiness (both at the beginning of the day, as well as coming back from breaks and lunch)
- Higher rates of employees calling in "sick" (over 33% of employees admit to calling in sick when they really aren't)[4]
- More grumbling and complaining from employees

- Changes in procedures are less likely to be implemented, and there is an overall higher level of resistance to change
- Higher rates of negative interactions occur between employees, both with their supervisors and their colleagues (typically, over "little" things)
- Lower customer and patient satisfaction ratings.

An interrelated (and interesting) result: *managers don't like their work as much when staff report lower levels of appreciation.* In fact, one study found that 81 percent of employees were just marginally engaged in their work, yet only 30 percent were thinking about looking for another job.[5] That means *50 percent*—half—of employees weren't fully committed to their job, but they weren't going anywhere else. Now that's a fun group to manage!

THE FALSE "KNIGHT IN SHINING ARMOR": EMPLOYEE RECOGNITION

Employee recognition programs have proliferated over the past two decades, to the point that global human capital firms report that between 85–90 percent of all businesses and organizations have some form of employee recognition program.[6] (Some of the programs may be as little as sending a form email on employees' birthdays but most are far more involved and fully developed.)

Good reasons exist for the focus on employee recognition. In the early days of recognition, employees were rewarded for work well done, demonstrating desirable behaviors (attendance, being cheerful when answering the phone), and for reaching established, measurable goals. Often the goals set had to do with productivity—reaching standards of output, reducing the frequency of errors, and, obviously, increasing sales.

Problems developed, however, when higher-level managers and financial analysts saw the benefits (in terms of profitability) to the company, and they began to create and try to implement more and more ways to incentivize (and recognize) employees to "do more." This essentially became a classic example of the belief that *"if 'some' is good, 'more' should be better, and 'a lot' should be great!"*

The result is that the large employee recognition programs (systems, policies and procedures, with electronic platforms) that have been developed have made recognition empty and meaningless. This is what I hear when I talk to employees *and* supervisors about their employee recognition program:

a) *apathy*: "I think we have a recognition program. Yeah, we do. You go down to the break room where they have donuts, do the same ceremony every time, and someone gets a certificate and a gift card. I don't go anymore, unless I stop by and sneak a donut."

b) *sarcasm*: "Oh, yeah, we've got a great recognition program. I was 'employee of the month' once, and part of the deal is you get a special parking spot for the next month. The problem is, I ride my bike to work. But I still got the parking spot!"

c) *cynicism*: "What a farce! It's all for show . . . they do it to make themselves look good to the board of directors. They don't give a rip about us. The award just rotates from one department to the next, and it is all about who the manager likes the most."

THE REAL ANTIDOTE:
AUTHENTIC APPRECIATION

In the book I coauthored with Dr. Gary Chapman, *The 5 Languages of Appreciation in the Workplace*, we share how appreciation can be communicated in ways that are meaningful. While employee recognition can be relegated to an impersonal process, appreciation—*authentic* appreciation—must be personal. That is, appreciation occurs between two *people*—not a manager and direct report, not from the HR director to the chosen "employee of the month," but between Shanya and Richard, or Juan and Stephanie.

Rather than restate the key aspects of the 5 languages of appreciation and the core principles upon which they are built, I will refer you to the resources we have created, used, and verified through research. Our cornerstone book, *The 5 Languages of Appreciation in the Workplace*, provides a thorough description and analysis of:

• the negative state of many workplaces and why they occur;
• the importance of appreciation in creating positive work environments;
• what the 5 languages of appreciation look like in daily work life; and
• how to identify each employee's preferred way of receiving appreciation.

The book also provides a free registration code to take the online Motivating by Appreciation Inventory.

Finally, let me emphasize that *we absolutely know how to train employees and managers to effectively communicate authentic appreciation*, and have done so in numerous settings (and across the world!). Our resources have been used by 70 percent of the top ten Fortune 500 companies, in over thirty different industries (including for-profit, not-for-profit, and government sectors), by over three hundred colleges and universities, and on six continents.

As you may already know only too well, not every organization jumps at the chance to personally, individually, express appreciation to their team. You may be part of one of those organizations. But with these proven strategies you can be the "change agent" to help build a healthier workplace—where people feel truly valued.

Section 1

HOW MANAGEMENT CAN CREATE OBSTACLES

This section focuses on the challenges that can be created by leaders in an organization, including: If you're in management, you may be part of the problem. Without buy-in from leadership at all levels, a commitment to applying appreciation in your organization will not succeed. In this section we look at management problems—and solutions:

- Chapter 1: a general lack of support for appreciation from management
- Chapter 2: the different types of pushback and resistance supervisors sometimes exhibit
- Chapter 3: the mistrust and negative reactions created by perceived inauthenticity

In each chapter, you'll find practical action steps for successfully overcoming the obstacles described.

1

YOUR LEADERS
AREN'T INTERESTED

Mark was getting tired of the meeting. As president of the company, technically the monthly executive team discussion was "his" meeting, but now he was feeling antsy and eager to get back to his office to deal with some pressing items. Too many decisions funneled through this team, he thought. It wasn't efficient. He looked at the clock and said, "Okay, what's next?"

Scott, the COO, responded, "One more topic and then a few housekeeping items. We are going to hear a report and proposal from HR on implementing an appreciation program for the employees."

"I thought we already had a fairly robust employee recognition program that costs us a pretty penny every year," Mark said in a not-very-interested tone of voice. "Why do we need something else?"

Debbie, the CFO, spoke up. "We don't. We pay our employees at a level *above* the regional average, and they have a pretty nice benefits package, even with insurance premiums skyrocketing. *That* should make them feel appreciated!"

"Well, we have Amber waiting outside," cautioned Scott.

"Let her in," said Mark.

Amber was the young, newly hired director of human talent management—"a fancy name for training director," Debbie had once commented. Amber came in and launched her PowerPoint presentation, sharing the results from the employee engagement survey that showed that a vast majority of the firm's employees did not feel valued or appreciated. She had done some research and found that this was the case for many companies within their industry, and that traditional employee recognition programs that focused on rewarding years of service or giving an occasional "above and beyond" award didn't really have much impact on most staff.

She then went on to offer some ideas on how managers and supervisors can communicate authentic appreciation. But what got the group's attention was her statement that "Appreciation pays off for a company. We have data that show positive results across the board—improved attendance, less turnover, more compliance to policies, higher customer service ratings." She offered appropriate supporting documentation and distributed an outline of her proposed plan to launch the appreciation training.

After Amber concluded and left the room, Mark said, "Well, that was better than I thought it would be, and it seems reasonable to at least explore the idea—maybe introducing it on a limited scope at first."

"I'll look into it," Debbie said. "The research seems a little 'soft' to me—but if the data supports the financial benefits she claims, then we can look at it." She then gathered up the materials and put them into her briefcase, where they were quickly "filed" after the meeting. The documents never saw the light of day again, and Amber never heard anything more about her presentation.

Whenever I speak to a group of employees, supervisors, or HR managers, inevitably I'm asked one or more of the following questions.

"What am I supposed to do if our management team isn't interested in appreciation? They are focused on achieving goals and the bottom line— they think communicating appreciation is stupid and a waste of time."

"Recognizing employees for anything (except for how many years

they've been an employee) is just not part of our culture. Any suggestions on how to introduce the idea?"

In an awkward way, this may be somewhat comforting—to hear that others often experience the same lack of interest or support that you do ("I'm not the only one!"). Conversely, it can also become discouraging if you start to think, *"Do you mean that hardly anyone is interested in helping employees feel valued and appreciated?"* In reality, a lot of business owners and managers *do* want to learn (and teach their employees) how to communicate authentic appreciation effectively.

But, at the same time, within virtually every organization, there are individuals who don't understand what we mean by "authentic appreciation" (usually confusing it with traditional employee recognition), or truly don't see the value of helping employees feel appreciated.

Sometimes leaders seem to want a positive, vibrant organization without providing the foundational components necessary to build one. Common responses fall along these lines:

"We pay them—that's how we show them we appreciate them. If they need to be praised for every little thing they do to keep motivated, they should find another job."

"THIS IS A MANUFACTURING plant. Tell them to go work for Apple or Google if they want to play Ping-Pong."

"I don't care if they feel good about themselves or not. My goal isn't to make them happy. My goal is to get the work done and out the door."

"I never got a pat on the back, and I turned out fine. People these days need to grow up and live in reality."

"We don't have the time or money. We're just trying to stay afloat. This is a manufacturing plant. Tell them to go work for Apple or Google if they want to play Ping-Pong."

WHAT LEADERS GET
WRONG ABOUT APPRECIATION

Many leaders, however, aren't opposed to appreciation. They just don't understand how it really works. In essence, they need accurate information about what communicating appreciation really looks like in daily work life, what it isn't, and what they can realistically expect appreciation to accomplish in their organization.

"Appreciation" has become a major buzzword in many workplaces —to the point that there have been numerous commercials in the media boasting "We Appreciate You" (often in the context of employees to customers).

In recent years, the emphasis has been more on employee recognition, with numerous books, articles, seminars, and even whole companies committed to helping leaders and managers recognize their team members for work well done. In fact, experts in human resource management estimate 90 percent of all businesses and organizations in the United States have some form of employee recognition program.[1]

The problem is—in terms of helping employees feel truly valued and appreciated—employee recognition programs have failed. While recognition and reward programs have proliferated, the level of employee engagement in job satisfaction has actually *declined* over the same time period. This is largely because most employee recognition activities are generic (everyone gets the same award organizationally in contrast to being individualized and personal) and, ultimately, come across as inauthentic.

As a result, many organizations are now focusing on emphasizing authentic, personal appreciation. While this is a step in the right direction, many leaders still have misconceptions about what appreciation is and is not. Here are the three major misconceptions we've come across.

MISCONCEPTION #1:
MONEY IS THE #1 MOTIVATOR FOR ALL EMPLOYEES

This belief is reflected when a leader responds to the suggestion of exploring how to effectively communicate appreciation to employees with the remark: "We pay them. That's their appreciation."

While we all need to make *enough* money to support ourselves and our families, many business owners and managers believe their employees are motivated primarily by making *more* money. This belief stems partly from leaders assuming that their staff is driven by the same motivator(s) they are—earning more money, enjoying nicer possessions, gaining social status, and having the ability to make decisions. (It is important to note that some leaders, often entrepreneurs and salespersons, *are* motivated by money.)

The truth is, *money isn't an effective motivator for many people.* And the research is definitive. When reviewing over ninety studies over a time span of 120 years, the results found that the relationship between salary level and job satisfaction is very weak—how much money employees make accounts for only 2 percent of the factors contributing to how much they enjoy their work.[2]

In fact, some research has actually shown that, in some cases, when financial rewards are increased, intrinsic motivation (the drive from within a person to complete tasks) actually *decreases*.[3] Employee engagement has been found to be three times more strongly related to intrinsic motivators than extrinsic rewards,[4] and intrinsic motivation is a stronger predictor of job performance than extrinsic rewards.[5] The point? *Motivating solely by money doesn't get you much.*

Another study, completed by the McKinsey consulting group, found that *non-monetary incentives were more motivating to employees than monetary rewards.* They found that praise from the employee's manager, attention from leaders, and the opportunity to lead projects were more motivating and rewarding than financial incentive, whether it was an increase in base salary, bonuses, or stock options.[6]

And these studies don't even address the differences in motivation among millennial employees—where research clearly shows just making more money isn't what drives them.[7] They are more focused on making a difference in the world, growing personally and professionally, and having a satisfactory work/life balance.

MISCONCEPTION #2:
THE PRIMARY GOAL OF COMMUNICATING
APPRECIATION IS TO MAKE EMPLOYEES HAPPY

This belief position seems to be held more frequently by individuals on the cynical side, who tend to say things like, "Work is about getting things done . . . I don't care how people feel about it."

Unfortunately, there is some basis for holding this belief. In the world of encouragement and positive thinking, some well-meaning individuals have taken the appreciation emphasis to the point of having a goal of making everyone happy. In fact, some workplaces have established the position of "Chief Happiness Officer."

As a psychologist, I can easily assert that attempting to make others happy is, and will always be, an endeavor doomed to fail. Why? Because no one can make anyone else happy. We actually can't even *make* ourselves happy! Happiness is a result of other positive habits in our lives.

We now know that our feeling responses are essentially a result of whether our expectations are met in real life. If they are met, we are pleased; if they are not met, we become frustrated, angry, or disappointed. Although we can assist people in learning to adjust their expectations more closely to reality and develop a greater sense of gratefulness, no one can make anyone else feel anything.

MISCONCEPTION #3:
THE PRIMARY PURPOSE OF COMMUNICATING APPRECIATION IS TO INCREASE PRODUCTIVITY

The third mistaken belief about communicating appreciation in the workplace has grown out of a distorted view of recognition and its benefits. When recognition experts and researchers began to share the positive financial benefits that occur when people feel valued, business leaders who were excited about the results started focusing primarily on the fiscal aspects.

Research has consistently demonstrated a strong return on investment in response to employees being recognized and feeling appreciated, including:

- increased daily attendance (not a small factor for retail stores and fast food restaurants);
- decreased tardiness;
- employees following policies and procedures more faithfully;
- reduced conflict among staff;
- increased productivity (in some work settings); and
- higher customer satisfaction ratings.

These benefits all add up to save companies money and make them more competitive in the marketplace. In fact, high staff turnover has been shown to be the single greatest nonproductive cost to businesses.

But when the *purpose* of appreciation is driven primarily (or in some cases, solely) by financial factors, the game changes. Some employees believe management is using the idea of "recognition" with the ulterior motive of increasing productivity, and therefore profits (and, not incidentally, manager bonuses). As a result, in the world of employee recognition we're seeing a huge pushback from employees and some managers.

THE TRUE PURPOSE FOR
COMMUNICATING APPRECIATION

What then is the real purpose of communicating appreciation for those with whom you work? Ultimately, this is a personal issue for each individual: *Why do I communicate a sense of appreciation to my colleagues?*

Multiple reasons exist, including some that are self-serving, but fundamentally, *appreciation for colleagues communicates respect and value for the person.* People are not solely "work units" whose primary value is derived from how much they produce (although some cultures, businesses, and bosses still view employees as expendable resources used to create financial gain, similar to burning coal to create electricity). Authentic appreciation flows from valuing employees as *people*—encompassing not only their capabilities and what they accomplish, but also how they enhance the work of the team and, finally, who they are.

It's important to note that the appreciation doesn't always have to be for the work they do. Some individuals are appreciated by their colleagues for just "who they are." For example, some employees brighten up the office because of their cheerful demeanor and positive outlook. Others are appreciated because of their calm attitude and ability to think through the issues in the midst of a crisis. And some are respected for what they do outside of work—a single mother committed to her family, an individual who gives a lot to the community through volunteerism, or someone who demonstrates self-discipline by training for a marathon.

Interestingly, when employees feel valued (whether or not the characteristic is work-related), good results follow. Not only do work-related behaviors improve, but employees who feel appreciated are easier to get along with—they are less irritable, more willing to listen, and more open to change. As hundreds of businesses and organizations have discovered, appreciation is a low-cost way to reward and motivate others, socially reinforcing the fact that what they do and who they are matters.

When appreciation is communicated from the perspective that

each employee has value as a person, in addition to the contributions they make to the organization, all stakeholders win—the employee, the supervisor, the organization, customers and clients, as well as the family and friends of the employee who get to enjoy a more positive, encouraged individual.

YOU GET IT, MANAGEMENT DOESN'T

You may be saying to yourself, "I get it. I agree! I see the importance and value of showing employees that they are appreciated, but my bosses don't. What you are describing is *not* how they think about employees. How can I help them see the value of appreciation? Can I? Is it even possible?"

To answer these questions, let's first look at and understand the nature of resistance.

Resistance to change (or a new program) can be displayed by team members at any level of the organization—the owner, executives, managers, supervisors, frontline employees. When individuals don't demonstrate much interest in learning how to build a culture of appreciation, or sometimes actively oppose it, their response can be accurately described as "resistance." Either actively or passively, they are resisting doing something new and different.

Different models have been developed to understand the nature of resistance, but one of the most practically useful has been proposed by Rick Maurer in his notable book, *Beyond the Wall of Resistance.* Maurer offers three primary reasons why people resist change:

1. "I don't get it."—a lack of information or understanding.
2. "I don't like it."—their emotional reaction to how the change impacts them.
3. "I don't like you."—a result of a lack of relationship and/or trust.[8]

Therefore, resistance to change continues to occur in organizations when the issues at each level have not been addressed. Sufficient information and explanation isn't given. Managers don't listen to and acknowledge the emotional impact of the proposed changes on the employees. A general lack of relational connectedness or a lack of trust in the management (related to their motives or competence) is present.

Maurer submits that resistance is usually only addressed at the informational level, with the proponents of change believing that if they explain the context and reason for the change factually, and how the change will occur, that should be sufficient. Typically, this approach isn't effective.

©Glasbergen
glasbergen.com

"Just the same, it's nice to get an award."

In fact, this ongoing resistance can irritate leaders. Jonathan, the HR manager in charge of employee engagement, complained: "What do these people want? We've told them why we want to launch this training. We've explained how it will make the work environment more positive for everyone. And I've outlined a specific process for how we can slowly phase this in over time. What else do they need?"

Many leaders believe successful organizations are the result of wise decisions and implementation, and that good decisions come from accurate information (which is generally true). Thus, they tend to focus on facts and data. But when dealing with *people*, simply having the facts isn't sufficient.

Resistance to change includes employees' emotional reactions to how their lives will be impacted and is also affected by the level of trust in relationships. A deeper resistance remains even when they understand the facts of the situation. For example, Erin reported to her supervisor: "I know this new direction and way of doing things makes sense intellectually. Eventually, the workflow will be smoother, there will be less confusion, and it should make us more efficient. But I still don't like it—partly because it feels like the changes are being shoved down my throat."

ALL OR NOTHING?

An additional problem related to resistance is the way that we talk about it, which is usually in "all or nothing" terms. When a manager isn't too excited about having his work group go through the Appreciation at Work training, the HR trainer may report: "He's against it" or "It's not going to happen—no way." Or if the manager is willing to pursue the training, the facilitator may state to her colleagues: "We're good to go. She's on board and it is full speed ahead!"

The reality in both situations is probably somewhere in the middle. The "anti-appreciation" manager may have some reservations, or feel now is not the right time. But to conclude "it's never going to happen" may be an overstatement. Similarly, the supportive manager may be willing to have her team go through the training process, but may have some unspoken qualms and eventually may not really support implementing the appreciation concepts over time.

Therefore, it can be helpful to individuals who are trying to convince colleagues of the benefits of using the Appreciation at Work resources to first of all not overreact, and secondly, to gain a clearer sense of what their coworkers are thinking (and why). See the diagram below showing the continuum of positions a leader could have regarding acceptance of going through the training with their team, and the words that may be used to describe their position.

Continuum of Resistance Responses						
Not Going to Happen	Highly Unlikely	Unlikely	Neutral	Possible	Probable	Definitely Will Happen
Not on my watch.	Maybe some other time.	If we have the budget.	Maybe next year.	Let's look at next month.	Check the calendar	Let's get it on the schedule.
We are not doing it.	I'm not doing it.	You can, but I'm not going to.	You can look into it.	Ok, if that's what you want to do.	It will be good for us.	Let's do it!

If your manager starts out highly negative, don't necessarily give up. Try to move her up the continuum a couple of notches. You are more likely to get into the positive response realm from a neutral position than a hardcore negative one, so try to slowly move into the neutral zone first. (Suggested actions for doing so follow at the end of the chapter.)

WHEN STAFF FEEL APPRECIATED, RESISTANCE TO CHANGE DIMINISHES

Laying a foundation of appreciation with your colleagues can go a long way in helping them approach organizational changes with a more open mind. Interestingly, when employees feel truly appreciated for what they do and who they are, resistance to change can be reduced significantly.

First, when employees feel positively about themselves at work, they are able to hear the information presented about upcoming changes more clearly. They do not have the extra noise of internal distractions that gets in the way of being able to listen and "hear" the facts presented.

A sense of feeling valued, even in the midst of significant organizational change, can help ease employees' initial emotional reactions. Responses of intense anxiety, fear, or confrontational disagreement become less frequent. Keira shared in a team meeting with her supervisor, "This whole 'change thing' scares me. I'm not sure if it will work and I'm afraid that eventually my job won't be needed. But, Lisa, I know you work for what is best for all of us and if you say we should do it, I'll go along even though I have my doubts."

FEELING APPRECIATED CREATES ENERGY FOR CHANGE

Resistance takes energy (if you're a runner, think about how tired you become after running on a windy day). Since each of us has a limited amount of physical and emotional energy, resistance consumes energy needed for other tasks, including implementing the changes themselves. When resistance lessens, more energy becomes available for constructive tasks.

Also, communicating authentic appreciation among colleagues injects positive energy into a workplace. People become more energized.

They have a greater capacity for creative problem solving and persevering through difficult tasks. Team members work together more effectively.

Over the past three years, we have worked with a division of a large telecommunications company in training supervisors and frontline staff in how to effectively communicate authentic appreciation to one another. The company was then acquired by another firm, triggering major changes across the whole organization. During the transition, leaders, both midlevel managers and upper-level executives, observed and repeatedly commented on how much more smoothly the staff who had been trained in authentic appreciation adjusted to the changes than the divisions who did not have this foundation established.

IDEAS TO GET STARTED

Okay, you're interested. But where do you start? To be honest, there are no magic formulas here. Nothing works *every* time. But we do have a few practical suggestions that seem to help.

First, *find out where you are (with regard to employees feeling appreciated)*. You can review the past year's employee engagement survey to see how your team responded to questions about feeling valued and appreciated. Alternatively, we have created a brief twenty-item rating scale that can be taken anonymously to assess the level of appreciation in a workplace (see it at www.appreciationatwork.com/aawrs). Or you can get input from key team members, talking with them individually: "What is your sense of how appreciated (or not) you think the team feels?"

Second, *begin to educate your management about the importance of appreciation* and how it can have a significant positive impact on numerous aspects of the organization (staff morale, attendance, turnover) and communicate authentic personal appreciation. Our book *The 5 Languages of Appreciation in the Workplace* has a chapter on the "ROI of Appreciation" and cites the research support for the financial and practical benefits organizations experience when their staff feels truly valued. Share some of the articles we have published in high-level business publications or in your industry area. Show them some of the testimonials we have gathered from leaders. Make use of the free articles and introductory videos on our website (www .appreciationatwork.com).

Next, have realistic expectations. Not everyone is going to be super-excited about the 5 languages of appreciation, or even showing appreciation at work, in general. Having said that, some approaches are more likely to win friends and influence enemies than others will. Be patient and work your plan over time. Don't expect rapid results (that is, until a directive is sent to improve staff morale due to the low employee engagement survey results!).

Share from personal experience. People (in this case, friends, co-workers, your supervisor, or others) are more willing to listen to a story about *you* than they are to listen to a bunch of factual information. If you haven't read *The 5 Languages of Appreciation in the Workplace* or you haven't taken the Motivating by Appreciation Inventory, don't try to convince others by saying: "I heard this was really good. You should read it." That leads to going nowhere fast. Rather, try something like: "I've been reading this book that I'm finding pretty interesting. It shows you that not everyone feels appreciated in the same ways." STOP. Wait. Don't go on and on for five minutes. Throw a bit of information out there and see if there is any interest or response. If not, let them take the conversation where they want to . . . or change the topic ("how 'bout them Cubs?"). If they show some interest in the appreciation topic, share a little bit more or say something like: "After I read a bit more, I'll bring it in and let you take a look, if you are interested." But keep your comments short.

Scatter some resources in their path over time. Have the book at your desk, where they might see it sometime. Subscribe to our blog and occasionally forward an article to them with a comment: "I found this to be interesting, and thought you might like to see it." Or go to our website and find the page that has some of our introductory videos and articles, and share one occasionally with them.

Begin to model showing appreciation to others. The best way to influence others is by our actions. If you really believe showing appreciation to others is helpful, start to do so with your workmates. You don't have to call attention to what you are doing. Typically, over time they will begin to notice your positive actions, and eventually may make a comment like: "You've really been supportive of me lately. I appreciate your comments and actions." Even if they don't ask you, "Have you been reading something that led to this?" this is a perfect opening to say, "I'm glad you noticed. I've been trying out some principles from a book I read. Can I share one of the main points I learned?" Be patient. They may not respond positively now, but they may come back in a day or two (knowing you won't "pounce" on them) and ask you to tell them about the book.

Gather together a few interested friends and begin to apply the concepts together as a group. It is difficult to model relational behaviors by yourself. Having a few colleagues work together can be significantly more impactful. Read the book together, take the Motivating by Appreciation Inventory, and begin to experiment in showing appreciation to one another in the languages important to each person. Talk about it together over lunch. Share what you are learning with your other colleagues. Often a bit of a buzz begins to build and someone brings up the topic in a staff meeting as a resource that the work group should explore.

Finally, don't try to get them to agree to a big project. Start with suggesting that you do a small pilot project with one group or department and see how it goes. We have found that starting small and building support and momentum over time is often the best strategy. There are a number of reasons this approach works well: a) you are really not asking your manager or supervisor to do anything, you are asking them to let *you* do something; b) you are not asking them to go "up the chain" and ask for some big, new program to be implemented; c) the cost (both financial and time) is relatively low; d) there is the potential that something good may come out of the process, in which case the effort can spread to other areas under their supervision, OR they may get credit for a resource that is a low-cost way to improve staff morale across the organization!

REFLECTION QUESTIONS

Why do you think some managers and executives aren't interested in appreciation in the workplace?

Which misconception about appreciation do you think is most prevalent in your workplace?

- ☐ That appreciation won't work because people are primarily motivated by money.
- ☐ That people are primarily focused on having a "happy workplace" (even if you don't think that is a realistic goal!)
- ☐ That the focus on appreciation is primarily to manipulate employees to work harder.
- ☐ Other _____

What reactions do you have to the statement that the primary purpose of communicating appreciation is to show respect and affirm the value of others?

What do you think about the idea that appreciation can be for "non-work-related" activities or for personal characteristics that don't necessarily improve work performance?

In your experience, which of the three primary reasons for resistance is the main reason managers resist pursuing appreciation in the workplace?

- ☐ A lack of information or understanding.
- ☐ Their emotional reaction to how the change may impact them.
- ☐ A lack of relationship or lack of trust.

When looking at the continuum of reactions to implementing a new idea or practice, where do you see leaders in your organization with regard to implementing the 5 languages of appreciation?

Not Going to Happen	Highly Unlikely	Unlikely	Highly Possible	Probable	Definitely Will Happen

Check the boxes you agree with.

☐ When people feel appreciated, their resistance diminishes.

☐ When employees feel valued, they trust others more easily.

☐ When team members feel truly appreciated, energy for creative problem solving increases.

☐ When employees don't feel valued, they are more likely to become discouraged and give up.

Which suggested action do you feel is most feasible for your workplace at this point in time?

☐ Complete an assessment to determine the level of appreciation reported by employees.

☐ Begin to share information about appreciation in the workplace with leaders and managers (articles, blogs, videos, chapters).

☐ Explore resources related to *The 5 Languages of Appreciation in the Workplace* myself and share what I am learning with others.

☐ Collaborate with one or two others to begin to apply *The 5 Languages of Appreciation* concepts in my workplace.

☐ Pursue setting up a pilot project with the Appreciation at Work training resources.

Consider using the Appreciation at Work Rating Scale[9] as a resource for this.

2

TWO BIG QUESTIONS
SUPERVISORS ASK

Brian and Anita were chatting in Yvette's office, discussing the recent announcement that came down from upper-level division directors. All three were department supervisors in different areas for the state agency that coordinates providing services to children and families, and each had worked for the department for at least five years.

"Well, what do you think about the directive for everyone to go through this training to teach us how to communicate appreciation to our team members?" Brian asked.

Anita was the first to respond. As usual, she was not shy about sharing her thoughts. "On the one hand, it sounds like a good idea. We know everyone is fighting burnout, if they aren't already there. With the budget constraints, you know we aren't going to see any raises and they aren't going to hire any more staff except to fill the empty slots by those who have left . . ."

"You mean, 'quit,'" Brian said.

"Yeah, whatever. But I'm not up for doing another 'flavor of the month' training that they roll out. We spend all this time, and then you don't hear anything more about it. It's a waste."

Brian laughed. "Then next year it will be another variety—'understanding your colleagues by what they wear' or something like that."

"The part that burns me," Yvette added, "is that yes, we should show appreciation to our staff, but who encourages *us*? We're coming in early or staying late to get everything done. We deal with clients who are usually mad about something. We hold our staff's hands to make sure they do things correctly. And I don't hear a thing from William or anyone else in management. Not a 'thank you.' Not a 'good job.' Nothing. And now we are supposed to just be all happy and appreciative to our staff? I just don't know if I have it to give."

Anita agreed. "I hear you. I'm there, too. Sure I want to create a positive atmosphere for my team. But as you say, what about us? None of us get much back from our clients . . . except grief. We're doing more with less. We're drowning in regulation. People think we're just bureaucrats shuffling paper.

"They can give us all the training they want. But will it make a difference? I don't think so, but . . ."

As we've already seen, many leaders do react negatively to the idea of authentic appreciation in the workplace. They aren't against the basic concept of being supportive to employees. But they wonder if such a program is "realistic." Our interactions with business and organizational leaders have uncovered two major responses that keep authentic appreciation from becoming a reality in the workplace. Let's unpack these.

REACTION #1:
"SO I'M SUPPOSED TO TELL THEM 'THANKS' FOR DOING THEIR JOB?"

I had the opportunity to provide training on how to communicate authentic appreciation to over 300 managers and supervisors of a group of long-term care facilities for senior citizens. In one of the sessions, we were dialoguing about the differences between authentic appreciation and going-through-the-motions employee recognition.

One of the supervisors asked, with a quizzical look on her face, "So I'm supposed to tell my staff 'thanks' for doing their job? That doesn't make sense to me. I'm more than willing to call attention to and thank them for doing 'above and beyond,' but I don't see why we should have to thank them for doing what they're supposed to do."

As the discussion continued, another leader asked, "What about those employees who want to be praised all the time, for everything they do? How are we supposed to handle those who were raised by receiving a 'Participation Award' just for showing up but not accomplishing anything?"

Interestingly, as the training sessions continued, a palpable tension grew between those who resent being told they should communicate appreciation for employees "doing their job" and those who believe that supervisors need to grow in their willingness (and ability) to communicate genuine appreciation to team members for doing their jobs well.

These concerns are not unique to this team of leaders. In a presentation to college faculty and staff, one senior faculty member stated bluntly, "This younger generation needs to grow up and realize they aren't going to be praised and get an award just for doing their job— that isn't the real world."

Both sides have valid points. And, like in most areas of life, a balanced approach seems wise. However, both sides of this discussion were becoming entrenched and attributing negative characteristics to the "other side."

In order to be able to pull out of the emotional quagmire that was developing, and to help proponents of each side be able to listen and be open to hearing a different perspective, I shared with the group the following example from daily home life.

"Let's say you are in a living arrangement—marriage, family, or with a roommate—where you agree to divide the responsibilities of daily life. And you agree to take responsibility for making dinner in the evenings and cleaning up the dishes. That's your 'job' in the home. You agree to it. It is not forced on you. And you dutifully carry out your responsibilities. Others accept responsibility for similar duties like vacuuming or mowing the lawn.

"Now, how many of you think it would be nice (and appropriate) to hear 'thanks' occasionally for making the meal and doing the dishes? Not *every* day, but at least every once in a while." (Nearly everyone nodded in agreement.)

"But, what if, over a period of time, you *never* heard 'thanks' from the others? Even though you agreed to accept the responsibility, and the other persons are doing their tasks as well, how do you think you may begin to feel?"

The group responded: "Resentful." "Taken for granted."

"But," I continued, "on the other hand, it doesn't seem reasonable to expect a big party and a 'thank you' card every time you make a meal, right? In fact, it's probably not realistic to be thanked every day for every meal, agreed? It would be nice but probably isn't going to happen."

"You've got that right!" said one woman about her family.

The tension in the room quickly dissipated, and we were able to continue to focus on *how* (not whether) to communicate appreciation effectively.

A losing argument: "what should be" vs. "what is"

Often, when issues and discussions are based in the values we as individuals hold, the discussion descends into an argument—either between two conflicting values of "what should be" ("They should be thankful they have a job!" vs. "But you don't have to treat them like slaves!"), or between "what should be" and "what is."

This latter discussion can sometimes be framed as between *idealists* (those with high ideals that they believe should not be compromised) and *realists* (those who look at the practical reality of day-to-day life and attempt to live out their values in the context of "what is"). While this dichotomy can become an oversimplification, the idealistic perspective and the reality-based perspective are both helpful, and needed. That is, if the argument is framed as an "either-or" problem, rather than a "both-and" challenge, no one will win the argument.

The reality: "yes, but with limits"

Whether employees (and supervisors and managers) *should* expect to be thanked for "doing their job" is actually a moot question. The fact is, they do expect it. Both personal experience and research demonstrate this reality. Monster.com, in surveying those who were looking for work, found that the number one characteristic job seekers desired in a workplace was *to feel valued by their employer*.[1] Recently, the Boston Consulting Group, in surveying over 200,000 employees worldwide, found that employees reported *the top reason they enjoyed their work was that they felt appreciated*.[2]

And it is well documented that when employees quit a job for another position, the primary driving force behind their decision is *not* money. Rather, they leave because they don't feel appreciated and due to interpersonal conflict with their direct supervisor.[3]

Additionally, as was reported earlier, we know that good things happen when employees feel valued. So, the answer to the question, "You mean I'm supposed to tell them 'thanks' for doing their job?" is— yes, you should.

"... but with limits"

But the flip side is also true. Work is about getting things done. That is what you were hired to do. And a supervisor's primary task is *not* to be giving continual praise and reinforcement to individual team members for completing their daily tasks. They do have other responsibilities!

Individuals who seem to be a giant sponge for praise and encouragement do exist—they never seem to get enough and are frequently asking (or hinting) for more. But, in reality, just like thirst, when you are thirsty, all you think about is getting a drink until you've had some liquid to replenish you. Then, after you get a sufficient drink, you quit thinking about wanting a drink (for a while, at least).

Similarly, when we communicate *authentic* appreciation in the ways that are meaningful to the recipient (reminder: it is not always verbal praise), then they are usually satisfied and don't need to be praised constantly. Many managers never experience this, however, because:

a) They are stingy with compliments and praise so their team members are always "thirsty";

b) The way they communicate appreciation doesn't connect with the employee; or

c) The employee doesn't believe they genuinely mean it.

The practical implications?

Don't get into the either/or mindset, where you argue with others about how much appreciation team members *should* want (or need). Remember, we are all different and none of us knows how much support or encouragement another person may need at this point (the amount needed almost certainly changes over time and life circumstances).

But also do not allow yourself to be put in a position of being emotionally blackmailed. Do not accept full responsibility for another person's happiness or sense of self-worth. You can't *make* someone else feel good. That is why I oppose "Chief Happiness Officers"—their responsibility is an unrealistic goal and a losing proposition.

As a leader in your organization (or a trainer to others), encourage those around you to:

• Do what you can to communicate appreciation to your colleagues.

• Learn how they like to be shown appreciation (it is most likely *not* the same way you do).

• Practice.

©Glasbergen
glasbergen.com

"If I walk past your desk without stopping to criticize your work, that counts as a compliment."

Finally, challenge them to a personal experiment: "Observe what happens when you consistently thank your team members for doing their work." I will bet a fair amount of money, they will begin to see positive results (if others believe they are genuine and the appreciation is communicated in the ways important to them).

REACTION #2:
HOW AM I SUPPOSED TO DO THIS
WHEN I DON'T FEEL APPRECIATED?

The second most commonly voiced argument from supervisors and managers is: *"What am I supposed to do if I don't feel appreciated? Where am I going to get the motivation and energy to show appreciation to my team members?"*

Interestingly, the intensity of this response is not typically as forceful as the "I'm supposed to tell them thanks" reply, and the topic is usually brought up later in the training process. The reaction is less defiant and oppositional, without the "You've got to be kidding me!" message implied.

The impression I receive from those asking the "what if I don't feel appreciated?" question is not that they disagree with the importance of employees feeling appreciated, but after a period of reflection, they honestly are asking themselves: "How am I going to do this when I feel discouraged myself?" They seem to be truly looking for an answer, rather than setting up an argument.

Even the CEO needs appreciation

The other intriguing aspect is that this response can come from anyone at any level in the organization—a frontline supervisor, a mid-level manager, the CFO, the receptionist, and even the CEO or owner of the business. Not feeling valued is not reserved only for "lower level" workers, which some people seem to assume.

While it is true that some positions in an organization have more prestige and influence associated with them—executives and managers are paid more, and some jobs are by nature more interesting and have other perks—the fact remains that ultimately *everyone* wants to know that they are valued by those around them.

One business owner and CEO of his company confided in me: "You know, the employees look at me and think I have it made. They see me speaking in front of groups, we have a big house, and we get to take nice vacations. It looks like the American dream to them. But they don't see the pressure I carry: finding enough work to keep fifty people employed or the fact that my personal assets are used as collateral by the banks, so if the business goes down, so do my savings. I'm not complaining; I have a good life, but it's

"EMPLOYEES LOOK AT ME and think I have it made. But it's lonely at the top."

lonely at the top, and no one seems to think that the owner needs to hear a little appreciation, too."

The problem with lack of support and encouragement for organizational leaders is *extremely* prevalent in not-for-profit, social service, or volunteer organizations. The burnout rate for directors of these types of organizations can be incredibly high. Why? Because usually the people the director reports to are "the Board" (did you hear that scary organ music play when you read that?). And the board of directors of a nonprofit or volunteer organization is not always the healthiest of groups. And understandably so. They are volunteers. The board members are usually busy, successful professionals, and while they may have a heartfelt passion for the mission of the organization, they typically don't have a lot of extra time and energy, let alone time and energy for encouraging and supporting the director or executive team. Result? The director doesn't feel valued or appreciated.

I'm not suggesting we throw a pity party for the leaders and executives of organizations, either in the for-profit or not-for-profit world. But we do need to pay attention and not assume that those at the top of the organization feel valued and appreciated. They too need to hear "thanks" or be shown appreciation in the language and actions they value.

I should note that showing appreciation to the boss can be seen by others as "sucking up." "You're just trying to look good to Sheri so she'll like you and give you the next team leader position that opens up!" The reality is, while this can be the case (either that the person is trying to gain favor by showing appreciation, or it is *perceived* that way), usually the truth wins out—that is, over time, a person's actions tend to reveal their real motivations. So I encourage employees to err on the side of taking the risk and communicating appreciation to those in higher job positions, rather than let their supervisor "die on the vine" because she never hears anything positive about what she does.

What can you do when you don't feel appreciated?

Ultimately, the issue comes back to the original question: *What, if anything, can you do when you don't feel valued yourself?* Just give up and gut it out? Look for another job?

Through interactions with non-appreciated workers, feedback from formerly discouraged managers, and suggestions by various authors, we've uncovered a variety of actions that can help when you feel unappreciated. Often, no one action solves the problem, but as a group, over a period of time, they can make a difference in your daily life experience.

Appreciation can start anywhere. One of the most exciting findings we have discovered in our work with groups across the world is that appreciation doesn't have to start at the top of an organization and then trickle down. Regardless of a person's position in an organization, they can begin to communicate appreciation to those with whom they work and start to have a positive impact.

The primary point is: *you can make a difference.* You don't have to wait for the CEO, vice president of HR, your supervisor, or anyone else. You have the ability to make a difference in your life and in the lives of those around you. This is opposition to the victim mentality that is sometimes fostered: "I work in such a terrible place." "Everybody is so negative." "I just feel stuck—there's nothing I can do."

Cultivate gratitude and thankfulness. Research has shown that individuals who keep daily track of things they are grateful for show greater determination, attention, enthusiasm, and energy compared to those who don't practice this discipline.[4] The same research found that even a weekly gratitude journal showed increases in optimism (and also a reduction in the report of physical ailments such as aches and pains).

Additionally, research at the National Institutes of Health found that people who show more gratitude in their life have higher levels of the neurotransmitter dopamine, which results in their being more pro-

TWO BIG QUESTIONS SUPERVISORS ASK

active in life.[5] Moreover, practicing gratitude creates a "positive snow-ball effect." When a person starts to cite things to be grateful for, their brain starts to look for more things for which to be grateful.[6]

Becoming more thankful in daily life doesn't take a lot of effort. Start with the simple things in life that we sometimes take for granted: running water, safe water to drink, food to eat, not living in a war zone, being able to see, hear, talk, and walk, friendships, family, and the ability to read. The list is endless but we sometimes forget all that we have and are blessed with.

Act positively in spite of how you feel. I'm not advocating for putting on a façade and pretending that everything is okay when circumstances are difficult. Yet we do know that when people choose to behave in certain ways, their feelings (both physically and emotionally) follow. So when you don't *feel* like exercising but you choose to start exercising, eventually you gain a sense of enjoyment from the activity. Or when you don't *feel* like going to a social gathering but choose to do so, often you find yourself being thankful that you did go. Similarly, interacting positively, with a cheerful tone of voice, smiling, talking about positive events, can create an atmosphere of positivity that everyone benefits from—including yourself!

Educate others about what encourages you. Sometimes people don't communicate appreciation because they don't know what to do. (This is one of the premises of the Appreciation at Work training—to teach people a variety of ways to communicate appreciation beyond what they typically know.)

One of the best ways to do this is to take your team through the Appreciation at Work training process, where you learn how each person in your workgroup prefers to be shown appreciation, and begin to implement actions to do so. Fortunately, in the process, they will learn how *you* like to be shown appreciation.

Similar to many people's personal experiences, your colleagues may be trying to show you appreciation but are doing so in a way that is not meaningful to you. So, sharing with them the ways that you *do* feel valued will help them hit the mark.

Ask for support. Leaders both teach and model desired behaviors. If you want others to share how they feel valued, then it is helpful for leaders to demonstrate this as well. In fact, one of the most difficult groups to engage in the Appreciation at Work training process is managers and supervisors. Sometimes they seem to believe that needing encouragement or support is a weakness, and they are embarrassed to admit that they could use some encouragement. It is my premise that life, including life at work, is difficult, and we all get worn out and discouraged at times. Therefore, it is normal for people to need emotional and relational support from each other. A healthy team knows how to support one another actively.

Look for small things. Sometimes colleagues and those around us are showing appreciation in small ways (a short "thank you," a smile, a nod of one's head, agreeing with a point you've made, or a simple "good job" at the end of a meeting). While these may not be as full and meaningful as the actions of appreciation we teach in our training, they are at least a start and should not be discounted or denigrated.

Keep a record of past encouragement and appreciation. There are times when we feel alone and think that no one values or cares for us. In these times our ability to remember the good times and the positive support we've gotten previously is difficult to pull up from memory. I myself keep an "encouragement file" where I have over the years placed notes of thanks and encouragement or printed out emails and texts with encouraging comments. When I need some encouragement and no one else seems to be giving it to me, I pull out my file and read comments from others from the past to remind me how people have appreciated what I've done.

Learn how to encourage and recharge yourself. Each of us differs in the way that we recharge ourselves emotionally. This can include experiencing nature, listening to music, exercising, having "alone time," engaging in a restorative activity such as reading or drawing, or performing a physical task like gardening or a craft. It is important to learn and discover the ways in which you become reenergized and make this a part of your weekly life.

Connect to your purpose. Sometimes the daily grind wears us down, especially when it seems like we encounter repeated obstacles to moving forward toward our goals. Reflecting on and reminding yourself about the purpose for your life, for your work, and how you are spending your time and energy can help sustain you when you don't know if you can keep going.

Look for and find support in other relationships. There are times when work-based relationships may be difficult and not very satisfying. (Hopefully this is not a long-term situation.) During these periods, it is helpful to keep engaged with friends and family and obtain support and encouragement from them. In fact, it may be important to let your friends and family know about your need for support from them *regarding work*, since currently you don't have a lot of support coming from your work-based relationships.

Determine whether or not this is a healthy workplace for you. Ultimately, if you feel virtually no appreciation or sense of being valued from others over a long period of time, then it may be important to consider whether this is a healthy work environment for you. In fact, this was part of the impetus for us writing our book *Rising Above a Toxic Workplace*, and also the pamphlet "How to Know When It Is Time to Quit Your Job." Although it may not occur very often, there are times when the best action to take is to leave.

> **THERE ARE TIMES WHEN leaders must lead, even when they don't feel like they have what it takes.**

Be a mature leader. Like it or not, there are periods of time when leaders must lead, and the mature must do what is needed, even when they don't feel like they have what it takes to do so. This essentially is at the core of maturity and leadership. Some people are able to step up and lead in these situations, while others are not. And we may be able to act and lead in some instances and not in others. I would encourage you, however, *not* to wait until you feel appreciated before you start to show appreciation to others. Otherwise, it could be a long time before you begin.

DON'T GIVE UP!

If your leaders really don't have the vision for trying to show appreciation to you and your staff, don't give up. All is not lost. People change. Circumstances change. And their opinions can change.

Remember, however, that just giving them the facts may not be sufficient (even if that is what they ask for). Go ahead and answer their questions regarding the ROI (return on investment) and what the benefits to the company will be. But remember that just providing factual information only addresses the first level of resistance.

Consider the following action steps, as well:

Ask questions to help you understand how they perceive the bigger context of the situation, what they think about your suggestion, and how they believe it may impact them. Don't just ask them, "Why not?" Ask questions like:

"Are there other projects or initiatives being considered that this training would interfere with?"

"What are the budget constraints we have to work within? Are there any other 'pots' of money we could access?"

"What concerns do you have about how having us go through this training would impact your responsibilities?"

Affirm and address their emotional reaction. Their reaction provides two valuable opportunities to build a bridge with them. First, you can affirm their reaction ("I understand, with all that is going on, this feels overwhelming to you") rather than arguing or telling them why they shouldn't feel that way. Second, their response gives you a window into how they are thinking about the situation. You then can brainstorm with them on ways to manage the perceived risks.

Minimize what it will cost them personally to move the process forward. Many times leaders automatically react negatively to new ideas because they don't want to take on any new responsibilities. If you can present your proposal in a way that shows it will cost them very little in terms of time and involvement, then they will be more likely to go along. Be aware of other potential "costs" such as reputation ("What if the training doesn't go well?"), intruding on their budget or other projects they had planned, the amount of paperwork to be filled out, or having to go to their supervisor to get permission. (Volunteer to present the information, with your supervisor being present.)

When possible, show them how helping team members learn how to communicate appreciation effectively will help them look good and/or tie into other company initiatives (employee engagement, staff morale). They may not immediately see how growing in appreciation dovetails with other priorities the company has been emphasizing. Give them ideas on how higher-up managers may like the idea.

INFLUENCE, LISTEN, MODEL

When team members across various levels work together well, good results follow, creating a dynamic atmosphere that promotes energy and growth within an organization. While no one can force others to agree with them or change their perspective, there are ways to influence others over time. Listening to their concerns, correcting misperceptions they may have, and modeling the behavior you hope to instill in others are good initial steps to take, and they will increase the probability of healthy interactions even in the midst of resistance.

REFLECTION QUESTIONS

To what degree do you find yourself reacting to the idea of communicating appreciation with "You mean I'm supposed to tell employees 'Thanks' for doing their job?"

Options:

☐ Not at all

☐ To a mild degree

☐ Moderately

☐ Quite a bit

☐ Fully and intensely

Share with others why you responded as you did (understanding that others may have different viewpoints).

Does the example of occasionally being told "Thanks" for making dinner at home affect your thinking on the issue? Why or why not?

Do you see yourself more as an idealist (having high ideals) or more of a realist (accepting "what is")? How do you think this affects your view of appreciation in the workplace?

Have you ever worked with someone who seemed to be a "black hole" for appreciation—you can never give enough? Do you think that most people are at risk for reacting to appreciation this way? Why or why not?

How prevalent do you think it is for leaders, owners, managers, or supervisors not to feel appreciated themselves?

What are your thoughts about the issues related to communicating appreciation to leaders? How realistic is the concern about employees using appreciation to manipulate their superiors?

If you ever find yourself in a situation where you don't feel appreciated, which of the following do you think would be most helpful to you?

☐ Accept the responsibility that you can make a difference and start to do so.

☐ Work on growing an attitude of gratitude and thankfulness.

☐ Take positive actions with others, hoping your feelings will follow and develop.

☐ Educate others about how you are encouraged.

☐ Look for the small ways that others may be showing you appreciation.

3

WHY RECOGNITION PROGRAMS DON'T WORK

Andrew knew what the guys in the room were thinking. The body language of the group was so clear no one needed to use any words to send the message: "That is a really stupid idea."

Andrew had just announced to the group of managers and supervisors for the manufacturing and transportation divisions that the company's executive team had decided that Andrew and his HR colleagues should take the division leaders through a training process to teach them how to communicate appreciation to the employees in their groups. Andrew knew this would be a difficult sell—not being sure how the 5 languages of appreciation were going to fit with this tough, "get it done" team.

Ed spoke first. "I'm going to tell my guys 'thanks' or write them a little thank-you note, and that is supposed to make them feel better? How about asking management to follow through on their promises they haven't kept—like getting us decent coffee and snacks for break time?"

Vince added: "Or raising the reimbursement rate for mileage (like they promised) when we have to drive our own vehicles to out-of-town worksites?"

"Give me a break," said J.R., one of the supervisors who had been around the longest. "What's the point? We know they're only doing this so we won't quit. It's like that stupid Employee of the Month program where you get a piece of paper and twenty bucks to spend wherever you want. Sure, I'll take the money, but most of the upper management doesn't even know what we do. They couldn't tell if I was doing a good job or not!"

Andrew had to admit to himself that most of their points were valid. The company generally had a pretty tough business approach in how they related to, and compensated, employees. And when there were individuals available to fill the slots when someone quit, the company was fine with just "rolling through" employees. But when it became tougher to find qualified, or even partially qualified, applicants, and the HR department couldn't hire replacements quickly enough, then management changed their tune.

Now the higher-ups were willing to do something more to appease the employees and, hopefully, slow down the turnover rate. So they found the Appreciation at Work resources and asked Andrew and his team to make it happen.

The problem was: nobody believed that it was the real deal. Neither the supervisors nor their team members accepted the premise that there was any genuine appreciation underneath the proposed training (at least from midlevel managers or above). Now Andrew sat in the meeting room, looking at these guys. He thought, *Sure, I could drag them through the training. But would it make any difference?*

Building a vibrant workplace requires a foundation of trust, respect, and honest communication. But many managers and employees are well aware of the problems with traditional recognition programs—how they breed cynicism and apathy and come across as a one-size-fits-all approach. I hear this over and over.

When I talk with employees, frontline supervisors, and midlevel managers about their companies' efforts to improve staff morale, usually through employee recognition programs, the most common responses I get are negative. "They don't care about us; they just do this recognition stuff to make themselves look good," said one employee.

"It's just a bunch of 'going through the motions,'" said another. "The people who give the awards don't even know who I am."

WHAT'S WRONG WITH RECOGNITION?

This doesn't mean there hasn't been a positive impact from recognizing employees' efforts and achievements. Research has shown the effects of recognition *done well* are decreased absenteeism, increased productivity, reduced staff turnover, and improved customer satisfaction.

While the prevalence of employee recognition programs has grown tremendously (in at least 85% of all organizations in the U.S. currently), employee engagement has barely increased at all (around 30 to 33% of the workforce report they are engaged).[1,2] So something isn't right.

Probably the most cynical environments I've experienced recently are medical settings and hospitals, public schools, and government agencies. Why might this be? It appears that in many of these institutions they've tried to communicate recognition and praise, or have provided training on "how to build a positive team," and it has been largely done through a program based approach, requiring everyone to participate. This leads, almost by definition, to a perceived belief of insincerity on the part of the participants.

When employees do not believe that others are genuine or sincere in their communication of appreciation, reactions include cynicism, lack of trust, disbelief, skepticism, resentment . . . the list goes on.

Why is this? Largely because people have not been communicated to with *genuine* appreciation.

WHY IS RECOGNITION OFTEN VIEWED AS INAUTHENTIC?

As I have explored the underlying issues with recognition, the following themes have become clear. Employees question the genuineness of recognition when it is:

- **Commanded.** Everyone has to participate whether they like it or not.
- **Organizationally driven.** The "recognition" comes from a divisional manager who has no relationship with the recipient.
- **Impersonal.** A lot of recognition is communicated to groups: "Way to go, team! Great job!" But the message says nothing about the team member who stayed late to make sure product would ship on time.
- **Generic.** The number of negative stories I have heard is amazing—like when everyone in a large organization received the same Christmas card with the same (low dollar value) gift card enclosed.
- **Fake.** When discussing reasons why recognition is seen as inauthentic, one astute (and brave) training participant stated: "Sometimes it's because they don't mean it."

If you're having problems in getting buy-in of your recognition program, you may want to investigate the perceptions of your employees and supervisors.

PUBLIC PRAISE AND OTHER THINGS EMPLOYEES DISLIKE

The way a lot of recognition programs are carried out helps feed employee aversion. Among them:

Public recognition. I ask groups, "How many of you would prefer *not* to go up in front of a group to receive an award or be recognized?" Regularly, 40 to 50 percent of the group raises their hand. (In some groups—administrative assistants, librarians—it's more like 80 to 90 percent.) One woman stated, "They can give me an award, but they'll have to drag me up there to get it!" If the purpose is to encourage an employee, shouldn't it be done in a manner *they* prefer?

Emphasis on verbal praise. While our research shows that using words to communicate appreciation is actually the preferred method for 40 percent of the workforce, there is a fairly large subset (20% to 30%) that doesn't trust words. Their mantras are: "Don't tell me, show me," or "Words are cheap." They believe in action and tangible proof. Many of these individuals don't want recognition or praise; they want help getting the job done.

I HAVE COME TO BELIEVE THAT the lack of genuineness in communicating appreciation may be the single biggest barrier to positive workplace relationships overall.

Reliance on rewards. Virtually every employee recognition program has a heavy reliance on rewards as a key component. Unfortunately, our research shows that *less than 10 percent of employees desire tangible rewards as the primary way to be recognized.* In fact, the percentage of those desiring tangible gifts as the primary way to be appreciated actually seems to be declining (from 10% in 2012 to 6% currently.) While most people like receiving some type of gift, if it is not also accompanied by sincere words, quality time, or helping them out, the gift is viewed as superficial and disingenuous.

SO WHAT SHOULD WE DO?

Ultimately, the question is "What should we do in response to this growing problem of perceived authenticity?" I think it needs to be answered at two levels: individually and corporately.

As Jim Collins stated in *Good to Great*, companies that are successful are willing to "face the brutal facts of reality."[3] If recognition in the workplace is viewed as superficial and fake, we better figure out why and then address the issues.

Unfortunately, some leaders seem to have the attitude of legendary comedian George Burns: "The secret of success is sincerity. If you can fake that, you've got it made." They want to act like they care about their employees. The problem is, faking it doesn't work, and undermines any trust the leader may have with their staff.

While we can't control others' perceptions, we are in control of our own behaviors and attitudes. Individually, we should each strive to be genuine and authentic in our communication with others—don't give praise when we don't mean it, and seek to communicate in the ways meaningful to the recipient.

Corporately, each organization needs to take a hard look at their recognition activities and take the time to obtain input and feedback from their staff about their perception of the employee recognition program and activities. Ask yourselves: Are there processes or procedures that foster a sense of inauthenticity? How much of our recognition is personal (vs. organizational), individual (vs. group-based), and communicated in the ways important to the recipient (vs. generic)?

Recognizing employees for the contributions they make to the organization is a good thing. But we are on a slippery slope that needs attention, lest our efforts crumble into a pile of devalued activities that will either be increasingly scoffed at—or discarded completely in the future.

WHEN "AUTHENTIC APPRECIATION" IS VIEWED AS INAUTHENTIC

The issue of inauthenticity is not limited to employee recognition programs. Even when trying to train staff in how to communicate authentic appreciation, employees raise concerns about the perception of inauthentic appreciation.

In fact, I have come to believe that the lack of genuineness in communicating appreciation may be the single biggest barrier to positive workplace relationships overall.

While the concept of authenticity is not that difficult to understand, there are some deeper questions that create some challenges —specifically in addressing the issue of perceived inauthenticity. Important questions need to be answered:

Who determines authenticity?

Is authenticity based in reality or perception?

What causes people *not* to believe others are genuine?

One of the challenges of the concept of authenticity is that it is, at least partially, based on the perception of the recipient. So you can truly value your colleague and be grateful for their input into the work process and try to communicate this to them, but they may believe you are just trying to manipulate them.

From my discussions with numerous groups, I've gathered a number of reasons why people question others' sincerity of communication. Let me cite a few:

• **Tone of voice does not match what they are saying.** Some individuals (stereotypically, engineers or computer programmers) can have a fairly monotone way of speaking and not show much excitement. If they are talking about how appreciative they are of you but say it in a flat tone, you may question how much they mean it. Or, some people may give a compliment with a sarcastic tone of voice such as: "Boy, it's great that you got your report in on time this month" (with the implication that this is the first time in six months that you've done so).

• **Nonverbal cues are incongruent with the verbal message.** Some people become quite anxious when speaking one-on-one with a colleague. They may have poor eye contact, a halting tone of voice, and seem tense while speaking. This may contrast with the message they are trying to send about how much they appreciate their coworker.

• **A sudden show of appreciation doesn't ring true.** If your supervisor starts to seemingly all of a sudden communicate appreciation and positive messages when they haven't done so in the past several years, you may ask yourself, "Where did this come from?" One trainee bluntly stated: "I haven't heard any appreciation for ten years and now you want me to believe they value me?"

• **Someone acts differently in front of others than they do when it's just the two of you.** It seems reasonable to question a person's genuineness when what they say to you personally (saying that they really enjoy hanging out with you) is not consistent with how they act toward you in front of others (ignoring you or even putting you down in front of others). Alternatively, they could compliment you in front of others but then ignore you and not interact with you at any other time. Likewise, saying things in private like "We should do coffee sometime!" then ignoring you when you pass in the hall sends up a red flag.

• **Inconsistent verbal messages over time.** Obviously, if there's an inconsistency between how they treated you last week (reaming you out for making a mistake or not meeting a deadline) and then complimenting you for the quality of your work this week—that leads to questions of authenticity.

• **Not addressing current (or past) conflict.** There are those we work with that we may have had an issue with in the past. Maybe their department did not deliver a product on time, which then put a time crunch on your department's ability to meet your deadlines; and you and their department head had a few heated words about the incident. If past conflicts are ignored and not addressed and communicating appreciation is attempted, this can create a clear sense of awkwardness.

• **You just took the class!** When a group in the organization has just completed their training in appreciation, it's normal for some to avoid expressions of appreciation for fear of being seen as insincere or trying out their appreciation efforts. (We call it "the weirdness factor.") This is a reasonable concern that has to be addressed.

• **Questioning the motivation of others.** Related to the above, sometimes we just question the motivation of others. Are they giving me a compliment because they mean it? Or do they have an ulterior motive? Or maybe they're trying to look good in front of others. And of course, we never can know with certainty because we can never truly assess another person's motivation.

• **When the recipient has baggage.** At times, the perception of inauthentic appreciation may not lie with the actions of the giver but rather stems from past issues the recipient is bringing to the situation. This can include a negative history with their supervisor or administrator, or with the organization at large—for example, they work for a hospital whose past efforts at promoting recognition failed. Or it may also come from prior work settings and having been "burned," which leads them to be less trustful in the current situation. And sometimes individuals bring *personal* history that distorts how they view others. For example, if a younger employee was raised in a family situation where their father would verbally communicate love or make promises, but then was rarely accessible and did not follow through, that person could have difficulty trusting adult male authority figures.

• **High expectations for oneself.** Some individuals have a hard time accepting praise from others if they have extremely high expectations for themselves. They feel like they're always falling short, so it's hard for them to believe that others view them positively.

These are all potentially valid reasons for questioning the genuineness of the actions from others in the workplace. The challenge becomes: *How do you get past perceived inauthenticity?* The answer lies, I believe, in first understanding the nature of authenticity.

AUTHENTICITY: REALITY-BASED OR PERCEPTION-BASED?

The issue of perceived inauthenticity in the workplace has become so widespread and deeply rooted that I have developed a more in-depth section of our training to deal with the problem.

Often, I ask participants: *Is authenticity reality-based or perception-based?* Consistently, the vast majority of individuals respond: "Perception-based." Only occasionally do I have one or two people say, "Both." And no one ever says it is solely reality-based.

I then share the following scenarios.

Scenario 1. "Can you truly appreciate a colleague, who they are or what they do, if they don't *believe* you appreciate them?" Yes, you can. Their lack of believing that you appreciate them doesn't change the reality that you truly do value them in your heart. (There are obviously numerous reasons why they may not believe you.) *So the appreciation is real but not perceived.*

Scenario 2. In a leadership training I was conducting on Appreciation at Work, I had a manager ask: "Why does the appreciation need to be authentic? If you can get the employee to *believe* you appreciate them, even if you don't, then the results will be the same." Initially, I was stunned. The thought of deliberately misleading others to believe you value them had never occurred to me. He went on to say, "You know, perception is reality, so if they just believe you appreciate them, that will get you the results you want." *So, in this case, the appreciation is not real, but is perceived to be genuine.*

I hope it should go without saying that our goal is both: we want appreciation to be reality-based and perception-based, because if we truly value a colleague but they don't perceive that we do, we have work to do. Conversely, our goal is *not* just to look like we appreciate someone. I do not want those using our resources to create *an image* of appreciation—we want to help supervisors and colleagues truly appreciate their team members and learn how to communicate authentic appreciation effectively to others.

At a foundational level, however, authenticity is ultimately reality-based. That is, a person either genuinely values another person or they don't. The ultimate judge of this belief is the person sending the message . . . and only they truly know what their thoughts and feelings are.

Unfortunately, this issue can go both directions. The worker may believe that their manager truly does value them, both for what they do and who they are as a person, but in actuality the supervisor is fairly talented at deceiving and manipulating others. Or, the recipient so strongly desires to be valued that they are easily duped by others.

As I work with teams and employees from a variety of settings, it is interesting to me that: a) rarely do we question our own authenticity; and b) most people feel like they are good judges of whether or not others are being genuine and sincere in their actions. That is, we generally give ourselves the benefit of the doubt—surely we truly value others when we say we do, but we are more likely to question others' authenticity and believe we are able to determine whether *their* motives are pure or not. This combination of beliefs concerns me because it sets us up to judge others critically while at the same time believing our intentions are unfailingly pure.

How can you prove your appreciation is genuine?

Given the issues described above, you can never fully *prove* your authentic appreciation, and you can't make someone believe you. Nevertheless, there are a number of practical steps you can take to effectively get past challenges of being perceived as not genuinely valuing your colleagues.

Only communicate appreciation when it is true. It is not helpful to try to fake it. People can pick up when you're being insincere. Similarly, it is not helpful for managers or supervisors to go through the motions of trying to communicate appreciation and encouragement just because that's what the organization is pushing at this point in time.

Acknowledge the barriers. Your team might appreciate honest statements like "I know I haven't communicated much appreciation to you in the past. . . ." or "I know we've had our conflicts and differences . . ." or "I'm not the greatest at communicating with others . . ." or "I know you may think I'm saying this just because we've had the training . . ."

State your desire to be viewed as genuine. Then you can follow up with statements like "but I hope you will believe me when I say that I do value . . ." Key to this is, the more specific you can be about what the person does or the character quality that you value, the greater probability that you'll be viewed as honest.

Be consistent over time. This almost goes without saying, but is critical. If you're "one-shot Charlie" where you communicate one message of appreciation every six months (and it is right after a training session!), the likelihood of being perceived as being genuine is low. Similarly, if you only communicate positive messages in ways or settings where it is evident to others (especially your supervisor or administrators), that communication also will lead to a perception that you're doing the actions just for show.

Don't focus solely on performance or on situations that benefit you directly. Employees become skeptical when the only times they are praised is when they have done above and beyond what is typically expected, or that they only hear comments about their "productivity." They then start to feel like cogs in a machine. Similarly, praising them solely when their actions bring some sort of benefit to you (for example, helping your department meet your standards and objectives, which will make you look good to your supervisor) becomes problematic. Alternatives include: commenting on their behavior when it is helpful to others in the organization, when it is beneficial to customers, or even beneficial to the community. And a very nice way to communicate authentic appreciation is to identify non-work-related skills such as treating others kindly.

Communicate appreciation consistently over time. The importance of this principle cannot be overstated, and that is why I'm repeating it. I believe the only true way to get past others' perceptions of whether our actions or statements are real is to demonstrate them repeatedly over long periods of time (months) and potentially in different ways and different settings. It is especially difficult for a recipient to argue that you are not being genuine when you try to find out the ways in which they are encouraged and seek to consistently and repeatedly communicate to them through those actions that are important to them.

THE FRUIT OF APPRECIATION

A healthy, vibrant organization begins to develop and grow—like new shoots coming out from the roots of a struggling plant—when authentic appreciation is nourished and cultivated. Healthy "fruit" such as positive relationships, improved work production, and quality goods and services are not far behind!

REFLECTION QUESTIONS

When you think about employee recognition programs where you have worked previously, what images or experiences do you recall?

When you see the list of common reactions (listed below) in discussions about employee recognition, which can you relate to? Share why you have the reactions you do.

☐ Cynicism	☐ Sarcasm
☐ Lack of trust	☐ Disbelief
☐ "I've heard it before"	☐ Wait and see
☐ Discouragement	☐ Anger

Which of the characteristics found in many employee recognition programs do you react to negatively?

☐ Commanded to do it	☐ Organizational and impersonal
☐ Generic	☐ Inauthentic
☐ Public in a large group	☐ Primarily verbal
☐ Emphasis on awards and gifts	

Which of the following sources of inauthentic appreciation have you experienced? Which bothered you the most?

☐ Tone of voice doesn't match what they are saying

☐ Words don't match their actions

☐ Behaving differently in public versus in private

☐ Inconsistency across time

☐ Demonstrating behavior not seen previously

☐ Not addressing current or past conflicts

☐ Timing (having just received training on appreciation)

☐ Past negative interactions with the person

☐ Questions about ulterior motives

What thoughts do you have in response to the idea that authenticity is both perception-based and reality-based? How might this concept affect your perceptions of others at work?

Have you ever experienced a situation where you questioned another's genuineness with regard to praise given to you? What was your response?

Did your perception of their authenticity ever change? Why or why not?

Have you ever had someone question your authenticity or motives in communicating appreciation to them? What was this experience like for you?

Section 2

WHEN WORKPLACE CULTURE STYMIES GROWTH

Section 2 focuses on the obstacles to a vibrant workplace that come from the work culture itself—issues that seem "baked in" to certain workplaces, including:

- Chapter 4: a pervasive negative environment,
- Chapter 5: a work culture of extreme busyness, with little or no margin for any activities besides the tasks at hand.

4

NEGATIVITY

Nancy is a nurse who has been at St. Mary's Medical Center for over twenty years. She has worked in a variety of units (pediatrics, general surgery, OB-GYN) and, like many nurses, she had worked the night shift, along with her share of weekends and holidays.

Currently, Nancy is the charge nurse for the day shift in the surgical recovery unit. Given her experience and commitment to quality patient care, Nancy could be described as a tough cookie. She tells you what she thinks, and she doesn't lack any confidence in her abilities and clinical judgment. As a result, she runs her unit with a firm hand and a straightforward, even brusque, way of relating to the staff (and sometimes the patients and their families).

When Nancy heard about the hospital's initiative to try to improve staff morale (and employee retention) through teaching them the concepts of communicating authentic appreciation, she laughed and said, "Yeah, right. Been there. Done that." In the midst of a staff meeting for unit leaders, she expounded on her view: "This is no different than when—four years ago, was it?—we went through the 'Write a Note a Week' campaign that petered out in less than three months. I think I got two notes, and none of the docs ever wrote a single one.

"The administration is always foisting these 'Smile and have a nice day' programs on us. What a waste of time. You can do this 'authentic appreciation' training if you want, but I'm not going to make my staff do it. If necessary, we'll sit through the training, but don't expect much from us."

Later, one of her friends, Janice, stopped by to chat. Janice, who was a charge nurse on another floor, said, "I heard about the new appreciation training they want us to go through. What a joke! I don't need to be appreciated—I need a raise! And they need to increase the differential pay for weekends, and give us back the employee discount at the cafeteria.

"If I didn't have so many years of seniority here, I'd quit in a heartbeat and go to one of those specialty outpatient surgical care centers. What a cushy job that would be!"

Nancy nodded. "This has got to be the worst place in town to be a nurse, except for maybe the county clinic. The administration here doesn't know up from down, and the docs treat us like we're at their beck and call. I'm just putting in my time until I can retire."

Just then, young, bubbly Angelica, the HR manager for the clinical staff, came by. "Hi, ladies! I just wanted to drop by and give you some introductory information about the Appreciation at Work training we will be doing. Don't forget to have your staff sign up for one of the training dates. I think it will be fun and encouraging! Well, I've got to run . . . have a good day!"

"Whatever," Nancy mumbled under her breath as Angelica bounced away.

When Angelica had gone around the corner to the elevators, Janice, in a chirpy voice, mocked her: "Have a good day! I appreciate you!"

Nancy and Janice snickered together.

Negativity in a workplace is like a toxic poison that slowly destroys an organization piece by piece. Whether displayed through caustic, cynical comments or a pessimistic, resistant attitude, negativity will "kill" (at least emotionally) team members over time, and any desire they have to help grow the organization will deteriorate.

A few years ago, while I was speaking on *Appreciation in the Workplace* to various groups across the country, I was surprised at the number of negative comments people would share with me during breaks and after the sessions.

"This appreciation stuff will not work here—this is the most negative place I have seen."

"I appreciate what you're trying to do here, but it will just be a 'one and done' event. The management has no interest in anything but maximizing performance and increasing profits."

"I agree that appreciation is important and I try to do the best I can with my team, but my boss will never go for it. He doesn't care about anyone else but himself and meeting goals."

This experience led us to investigate the issue further and eventually share our findings in *Rising Above a Toxic Workplace*. Fortunately, both through that research and our work with the Appreciation at Work training process, we've seen how authentic appreciation can significantly improve staff morale—leading to a healthier workplace.

To gain a deeper understanding of negative forces in the workplace, we are going to look at: a) the different types of negativity in the workplace; b) where the negativity comes from; and c) the antidote to help make the environment more positive.

WHAT DOES NEGATIVITY LOOK LIKE?

There are many ways negativity manifests itself in a workplace. Here's what I've found. You will probably recognize some or all of these!

Frustration and anger

Visit any workplace and at some point you'll hear someone say. *"I am so frustrated!!"* Managers, supervisors, and employees all get frustrated when things don't go as they believe they should. Equipment that doesn't work, clients who don't make decisions, coworkers who don't respond to important emails, vendors who don't get materials to you by the time they said they would—all are sources of frustration.

In the American culture, the word *frustration* actually has two primary meanings. First, frustration often means "blocked." We feel frustrated when we are trying to move toward a goal and encounter an obstacle that interferes with being able to achieve that goal. A second, and more commonly used, meaning of the word is irritation or even anger. So it is important to clarify when someone says they are frustrated: is it because they are feeling impeded from reaching a goal they are pursuing, or is it a nice way to say that they're angry about the situation?

Grumbling and complaining

One of the "news alerts" I share in my trainings is that when people don't feel appreciated, they don't keep it to themselves. That is, when people have negative feelings about what is going on, they tend to share them with others. This obviously can create a negative cycle of events, leading to others joining in with their own negative comments, and possibly even raising the intensity by the words they use (moving from "This is irritating" to "I'm so mad I could punch him out"). Research has repeatedly shown that when groups of people get together and start to grumble, negativity is fueled and things get worse.

> **WHEN PEOPLE DON'T FEEL appreciated, they don't keep it to themselves.**

Sarcasm and cynicism

When speaking to groups around the country (or in different cultures) I often tease, "So, is sarcasm part of the Southern culture?" Always my comment is responded to with significant laughter. Sarcasm seems to be a universal language (and I often note it is not the sixth language of appreciation!).

Sarcasm has been defined as the use of irony to mock or convey contempt. That is, sarcasm is a means of using words to actually say the opposite of what you want in order to show your irritation. Examples of sarcastic remarks in the workplace might include:

"Look who decided to grace us with his presence for our meeting."

"Well, we all know that Kim always gets her paperwork completed and turned in on time."

"Here's an example of the great communication that occurs from management when they make a decision that involves us."

Essentially, sarcasm is a way to indirectly communicate a negative message to others.

©Glasbergen
glasbergen.com

"No matter how busy I am, I'm never too busy to stop and complain about how busy I am."

Cynicism goes beyond sarcasm, stemming from the belief that people are motivated primarily by self-interest and are not honest about their agenda. Cynical remarks tend to have a sharper edge to them, with the intent of being cutting and hurtful. Cynicism is driven largely by skepticism and distrust. One example might be, *"Well, we know the management always makes decisions in the best interest of the customer and their decisions have nothing to do with increased profitability."*

Blaming and making excuses

This familiar pattern is less overt than other negative behaviors—but it can be more insidious. When employees blame and make excuses, it contributes to the overall negative work environment. This is because when people blame and make excuses they are not accepting any responsibility either for their actions or for corrective steps to solve the problem. Blaming focuses on other people: *"Well, I didn't get the information from Jerry until late last night,"* while excuses tend to focus more on circumstances: *"Sorry I'm late—the traffic on I-7 was terrible!"* while failing to mention that she also left home a half-hour late. When a large-scale pattern of blaming and making excuses exists within an organization, it clearly inhibits the ability to find out the source of a problem and to make corrective actions. Therefore, the negative patterns and problems may continue.

Discouragement and apathy

Over time, people get worn out from fighting workplace battles. Poor communication, lack of trust, and a sense of powerlessness lead to a general sense of apathy (*"Why try? We've been down this road ten times before"*), which ultimately leads to passivity by team members. So people give up and nothing gets solved.

Sabotage, violence, and bullying

While relatively rare, when individuals become so angry about a situation that they feel the need to react in some way, this can involve direct sabotage of a policy, procedure, or even a product—actively undermining the process or damaging products before they are shipped. And unfortunately, workplace violence does occur when a disgruntled employee reacts by destroying property or becoming violent against a coworker.

A subset of this behavior is workplace bullying—verbal and sometimes physical intimidation and threatening of others so the bully can get what he wants or just exert power over others.

WHERE DOES NEGATIVITY COME FROM?

To put the issue straightforwardly, people have negative reactions when their expectations are unmet. We each have expectations about our work life: how long it should take to get to work, what resources should be provided so we can complete our work, how other people (coworkers, supervisors, customers) should respond to our actions, and so forth. Many, if not most, of us can indulge in unrealistic expectations about work (our efforts will always be recognized, we will always have a good day, the work will always be meaningful). When our expectations inevitably go unmet, we can respond in frustration, anger, disappointment, and discouragement. Or we become apathetic and shut down, contributing the minimum. Or we gossip and criticize and undermine team unity.

A simple, practical way to think of expectations is that they are the "shoulds" (and "shouldn'ts") that we bring to specific situations. When those shoulds are met or fulfilled, we're pleased. When they are not met or when somebody does something they "shouldn't," we are not happy.

In my experience, a lot of negativity in the workplace comes from unrealistic expectations individuals have—that the photocopier should work every time, that customers should make a decision to buy your product (now), that your coworkers should always be friendly and glad to see you. These unrealistic expectations seem to come from two sources: a lack of experience related to the current situation, and an overall idealism about work.

When people are in a new job or situation, they may not understand what realistic expectations are appropriate for a customer's response or the time frame in which someone will get back to them. Similarly, it seems our culture has created some unrealistic and idealistic expectations about work (that it should always be fun or fulfilling)—which, as we all know, doesn't always match reality.

Some people take a very prideful, arrogant attitude toward their work and their coworkers. Genuine pride about a job well done is one thing, but some folks seem to think they could do the job better than anyone else (even though they have never done it before), or they secretly think, *"We should have done it the way I told you to."* And we've already seen the damage a passing the buck, "it's not my job" sort of mentality can do in a workplace.

Trust—or lack thereof—is a huge issue in many organizations, large and small, for-profit or not, public or private. So rampant is this problem that we have developed a series of training programs that address the issues of mistrust, lack of respect, and poor communication.

THE POSITIVE ANTIDOTE

Fortunately, there are ways to combat negativity in the workplace. We don't have to just live with it. I found that four specific actions can significantly (and fairly quickly) turn around a negative work environment.

First, ***don't participate in negative interactions.*** Not fueling the fire is an important step that many seem to miss. Just the simple step of not adding your sarcastic remark to a team meeting or not engaging in a small group informal complaint session among colleagues can make a difference. It's very tempting to pile on in a hallway or break-room conversation. Resist!

Secondly and simply, ***stay positive.*** Simply having a positive attitude about life (*"Isn't it a beautiful morning?"*) and having a cheerful demeanor can make a big difference. It is difficult for others to continue in an angry conversation when a workmate is there making positive, constructive comments.

Cultivate gratitude. Decades of research have demonstrated the impact of thankfulness on mind and body. We could devote whole books to the things each of us can be thankful for. Gratitude helps us feel less entitled and more aware of the blessings we've been given. Simply put, it makes us better people.

Fix it! Many negative reactions are in response to problems that occur. Sometimes, having a proactive "let's figure out how to fix this so it doesn't happen again" attitude can be quite beneficial. First, it gives people hope that this situation won't remain or repeat itself. Secondly, it infuses a degree of energy that is going in a positive direction rather than spiraling down into "life is terrible and this place stinks."

THE NEUROSCIENCE OF APPRECIATION

Not only does gratitude bring practical benefits to organizations, but there is physiological research to demonstrate how appreciation and gratitude benefit us individually as well. Recent advances in the ability to study the brain, neurochemistry, and neural pathways have made it possible to gain greater clarity on what happens in the brain when people feel genuinely valued.

The brain is driven by two systems: chemical (neurotransmitters—chemicals that help the nervous system communicate) and electrical (so we can "read" the electrical impulses in the various parts of the brain).

Dopamine is the neurotransmitter related to appreciation and its impact on an employee's behavior. Dopamine has been found to be the "reward and punishment" transmitter, so when an employee feels valued, dopamine is released in the brain. What happens next is really the important part: the dopamine then travels along a pathway that triggers motivation, the desire to act so that a positive result will happen.[1] Research at the Wharton School of Business at the University of Pennsylvania found that a simple "thank you" to employees increased desired work-related behaviors by 50 percent when compared to those who received no thanks.[2]

Not only does genuine appreciation increase dopamine, but when expected praise *doesn't* occur, then dopamine levels drop—which leads employees to avoid tasks for which they don't receive any thanks.[3] And even if a manager is purely self-interested, research shows that having an attitude of gratitude in one's daily life creates positive physiological effects (more balanced metabolism, improved sleep, less experienced stress) in the person who is *appreciative* of those around them.

ROOTING OUT THE TOXINS

Like a diseased tree that has bugs eating its roots and the inner bark that carries nutrients to its limbs, leaves, and developing fruit, unchecked negativity will destroy a workplace from the inside out. Teaching team members how to communicate *authentic* appreciation and to disassociate from negative interactions are two proactive steps that will root out these toxins and lead to a healthy turnaround in workplace relationships.

REFLECTION QUESTIONS

When you read about the level of negativity in workplaces, does this surprise you? Why or why not?

When reviewing the different types of negative experiences listed below, which ones do you experience? Which ones do you see most frequently at your workplace?

	You	Others at Work
Frustration and anger	☐	☐
Grumbling and complaining	☐	☐
Sarcasm and cynicism	☐	☐
Blaming and making excuses	☐	☐
Discouragement and apathy	☐	☐
Sabotage and violence	☐	☐
Bullying	☐	☐

Since negative reactions are a result of unmet expectations, what expectations do you have about your work situation that aren't being realized? What expectations do you see colleagues have that lead to their negative reactions?

Which of the following actions do you think would be most helpful to you and your colleagues in decreasing the negativity in your workplace?

☐ Don't participate in negative interactions.

☐ Have a positive attitude toward life in general.

☐ Display an attitude of gratitude.

☐ Be proactive in problem solving.

What action(s) would you like to commit to implementing in the coming weeks?

5

BUSYNESS

Michelle had a problem. She sat in her office looking at the Excel sheets that graphically laid out the dismal results of the annual "employee engagement" survey. Michelle, the director of HR in the company, knew something had to be done. Raises had been minuscule or nonexistent the last several years; the organization was only now beginning to recover from the economic downturn that had wiped out several of their competitors. Staff cutbacks had meant that everyone was doing more with less. She was aware of grumbling in hallway conversations, and the numbers on the screen confirmed the sense that morale was low across the organization.

Michelle's boss and others on the leadership team had given her and her colleague Lori, one of the corporate trainers, the responsibility of finding a resource (preferably at low cost) that would help managers turn around the negativity and boost engagement. Lori, always upbeat, had said to her earlier that day, "I'm really excited about jumping into this appreciation training! We need help in making our team members feel valued. They work so hard, and times have been tough the past few years so we haven't been able to compensate them as they deserve."

But how were department managers supposed to fit all this in? Michelle had voiced her concerns to Lori: "One of the problems is, everyone is busy. *Really* busy. Look at me. I'm here at seven and leave at six. Some of our people have to come in on weekends to provide additional coverage. In HR it is all we can do to just keep the positions of the frontline employees filled. The work is tough and the pay isn't great, so people tend to quit and find another job, which leaves the rest of us scrambling."

Lori nodded. "We can't shut down a department and have everyone go through the training at the same time. So we have to take a few employees from a number of departments and have them go through the training together. We're working on figuring out that scheduling challenge."

Michelle added, frowning, "But, secondly, and more importantly, I'm worried about a major pushback from both supervisors and managers. One already told me, 'How are we supposed to have the time to tell people we appreciate them when we barely have the time and energy to get the basics done? I like the idea, but I don't see how I can ask my team members to do any more.'"

Lori concluded: "He's right. People are working as hard as they can. But we need this."

Otherwise, Michelle thought, people will just quit, or stay and get burned out and frustrated. They had to make this work . . .

Seventy-nine percent.

Seventy-nine percent of employees who quit a job voluntarily cite a lack of appreciation as one of the primary reasons they leave.[1] And why is there a lack of appreciation? I can clearly state that—repeatedly, consistently, and regardless of the type of work setting—the #1 reason people report that appreciation is not communicated more is *busyness*. This is true in for-profit businesses, government agencies, not-for-profit organizations, medical facilities, schools, and every industry I've worked with.

Training participants report time and time again that they believe the *primary reason appreciation isn't communicated more is because people don't have the time available to do so.* And this is true no matter the position—executive, manager, supervisor, or frontline employee.

In fact, in one workshop, we started to go on to discuss the other reasons that appreciation isn't communicated more, and one individual spoke up and said: "No, Dr. White, you don't understand. Busyness is both the #1 *and* #2 reason appreciation isn't shared more! We are just *too* busy and we don't have time."

I get it. Rarely in today's world of work is anyone looking for more work to do. (Unless you are a night-shift security guard at a factory in a small town.) And I know people are not looking for more items to put on their to-do list—or lists.

And I promise our trainees (and you) that our goal is not to create another "Recognition" or "Appreciation" to-do list. None of us need that.

REDUCING UNNECESSARY BUSYNESS

Busyness, especially unnecessary and unproductive busyness, is like the unhealthy rapid growth that can happen in living organisms like plants. Busyness eats up resources (time, energy, money) for activity that may not be healthy for the organization or its members.

As a psychologist, I'm supposed to know something about behavior change, and how to help people change patterns of behavior and habits. One of the factors that we know improves the likelihood of changing behavior is if the *new* behavior is closely related to an *existing* behavior. So, for example, if you want to start an exercise program, you are more likely to be successful if you start doing an exercise that either you have done previously (e.g., jogging) or the new behavior (walking) is close to the previous habit. Therefore, if you were a jogger in the past, you probably will struggle more in trying to start swimming laps.

Similarly, in the area of appreciation, our goal from the beginning has not been necessarily to create totally new ways of relating to your colleagues, but rather *to slightly change what you are already doing in a way that it will be more effective*. That is the power of the 5 languages of appreciation. We are able to help supervisors and colleagues identify the actions that actually truly communicate appreciation to each individual colleague instead of trying a shotgun approach where you do one action for everyone.

YOU DON'T HAVE TO CREATE totally new ways of relating to your colleagues. But you can slightly change what you are already doing in a way that it will be more effective.

Not everyone likes verbal praise. Not everyone wants to spend time with you. Not everyone wants help on tasks. Not everyone wants a gift. And clearly, not everyone wants physical touch in the workplace.

But employees exist who desire each one of the different languages. And when we help individuals who work together find out not only the *language* of appreciation their coworkers prefer but also the *specific actions* that make them feel valued, then we can help everyone more easily hit the mark. This is better than wasting a bunch of time and energy doing all kinds of things that don't have any impact on most of the people.

As a leader trying to implement change, if you don't address the issue of busyness up front, you will continually battle resistance from others along the way. But if your audience knows you are aware of the issue, and are trying to help them in ways that will not only not increase their level of busyness, but also potentially decrease how busy they are, they will listen to you.

Our goal is to help supervisors and coworkers learn:

- who in their work group likes to receive an occasional encouraging email;
- who feels valued when someone stops by to see how they are doing;
- who enjoys and feels validated when they work together on a project with others;

- who is encouraged when someone brings in their favorite specialty coffee or other snack; and
- who enjoys the camaraderie of sharing a high five when a project is successfully completed.

Then supervisors don't have to send an email blast to everyone or stop by every person's desk. We help workers quit wasting time and energy doing things that their coworkers don't value (and even, sometimes, dislike!). By discovering what is important to different coworkers, then managers, supervisors, and colleagues can be more efficient and effective in their actions.

A top recognition manager for a large multinational corporation, who helped bring our resources to thousands of their employees, reported:

"One of the core strengths for the Appreciation at Work process is that it is easily implemented. The resources are adaptable to different settings and roles, being able to be used by frontline employees, supervisors, and managers immediately."

APPRECIATION: NOT BY SUPERVISORS SOLELY

Most traditional employee recognition programs historically have placed a lot, if not all, of the responsibility for recognizing good work of their team members squarely on the shoulders of managers or supervisors. This is unfortunate and actually creates unwanted negative effects.

Clearly, calling attention to work done well by employees is a good habit to practice. When staff feel valued for the contributions they make, a sense of loyalty and emotional engagement to the mission of the organization develops. But focusing solely on managers and supervisors to support and communicate appreciation to their staff often is an unrealistic expectation that creates problems:

- the manager feels overly burdened with trying to show appreciation to all members of their team;
- members of the team become frustrated with their supervisor when they don't feel they receive enough recognition for the work they do;
- the supervisor can become discouraged with their inability to encourage all team members consistently;
- an overall negativity and disappointment can develop in spite of the supervisor's attempts to be positive and encouraging toward their colleagues.

©Glasbergen
glasbergen.com

**"I'm sending you to a seminar to help you
work harder and be more productive."**

As a result, the second major way we address the busyness obstacle is to emphasize that *communicating appreciation is not just the responsibility of supervisors and managers.* This is actually a change from how we started applying the 5 languages of appreciation. Initially, we were focused on managers and supervisors, teaching them about the 5 languages and the importance of appreciation.

But fairly quickly, as we were working with various teams, we began receiving feedback that helped us see the need to alter our approach. After a training session, one administrative assistant asked me: *"Dr. White, I have a colleague that I want to learn how to encourage and support. We do essentially the same tasks but in different locations. We often work on projects together, and she seems pretty discouraged. I try to do what I can to help encourage her, but it doesn't seem to help. In fact, sometimes she gets* more *agitated and irritable. I'd like to learn how to use the 5 languages of appreciation to help her."*

Other employees also began asking if, and how, the concepts and the results from the Motivating by Appreciation Inventory[1] could be used to show appreciation to coworkers, and even colleagues in different departments. As a result, we developed the MBA Inventory Group Profile to help in this process.

When we added the ability to identify specific actions to the inventory, we then also created the MBA Inventory Action Item Template which provides a format to copy and paste the specific actions from each person's inventory report, so all team members can have a list of the appreciation actions valued by their colleagues. Creating these resources and incorporating them into the Appreciation at Work training process has been extremely helpful for coworkers who want to share appreciation with one another.

And if a supervisor or manager is not that "jazzed" about communicating appreciation, this provides a way to take initiative on your own—and help the organization.

MANAGERS SHOULD COMMUNICATE APPRECIATION, BUT . . .

Just to clarify, we are *not* proposing that managers should give up in their attempts to show recognition and communicate appreciation to their team members. We know that good results follow when employees feel appreciated by their supervisors.

But it has become increasingly clear that employees need to feel valued by both their supervisors *and* their colleagues. In fact, when employees and supervisors consistently and effectively communicate appreciation to their colleagues, positive results occur more quickly, are more dramatic in their intensity, and the staying power of their effect is longer lasting.

The result? Positive communication and improved morale to a level we never imagined!

Appreciation from a coworker can be as simple as a *"Thanks for getting that report to me quickly, Ann—that is really going to make it easier for me to pull together my presentation without having to rush at the last minute."*

When team members feel valued not only by their supervisor but also by their colleagues—and when they accept responsibility to encourage and recognize the good work others are doing—a positive "snowball effect" occurs that can become virtually impossible to stop.

I want to emphasize again, however, that shifting *full* responsibility to peers from managers is not a good idea. Managers need to lead by example, modeling acts of encouragement to their team, as well as provide the training and resources for coworkers to learn how to effectively communicate genuine appreciation to one another. (Otherwise, the "Do as I say, not as I do" approach will lead to increased cynicism and resentment toward the manager.)

WHEN YOU'RE IN SURVIVAL MODE

Some organizations really are just barely hanging on, with no margin for anything except ensuring their survival. One leader asked me, *"Yeah, but what if everyone truly is overwhelmed and just barely keeping their head above water? We genuinely feel like we are in survival mode. Should we just give up trying to show appreciation to each other?"*

There are times and seasons in an organization's life when people are working as hard as they can, seemingly for as long as is humanly possible—just to try to get past a crisis or help the organization survive. (This is, or should be, different from organizations or departments that run from one crisis to another due to poor planning, decision making, or implementation.)

I had the opportunity to work with an internationally known non-profit organization that, due both to the economic downturn of 2008–2010 and other internal factors, was reeling. They had already reduced staff by almost 50 percent in response to the significant reductions in charitable contributions, and they were still trying to right the ship.

After conducting a half-day training session with a large number of division managers and departmental supervisors, one manager bravely asked the questions introducing this section.

To be honest, seeing both the exhaustion and desperation in her eyes, I had to pause and gather my thoughts before I responded. I didn't want to just give a glib "Well, do the best you can" answer. Neither did I want to encourage her or other leaders to totally abandon the process of trying to show appreciation and encourage their team members—because that didn't seem to be a healthy direction, either.

I responded to her, and the group:

"On the one hand, we have to be realistic. Right now, you and those in your organization don't seem to have the bandwidth (emotionally or time-wise) to implement the concepts as we have been discussing—having supervisors take the MBA Inventory and having your HR managers take work groups through half-day training sessions.

"On the other hand, I don't think you should throw the baby out with the bathwater and do nothing at all. Rather, I would suggest you do what you can individually—being grateful to one another as you work together on tasks, and try to do so in the appreciation language important to them. (Everyone here has already taken the MBA Inventory, so you have those results.) A little encouragement and support here and there, even if it is inconsistent, is better than none at all."

They seemed to accept my advice, and implemented it. Eventually, they *were* able to get to the point where they started conducting Appreciation at Work training with their teams and implementing the concepts across the organization.

"WHAT IF I'M MANAGING FIFTY PEOPLE?"

The second major obstacle that is raised occasionally has to do with having a large number of employees on your team. The following was communicated by a supervisor in a manufacturing firm, but I have heard similar comments from other settings, especially in healthcare:

"Your approach seems fine for smaller work groups, say from 8 to 15 employees. But what do you do when you have 40 or 50 people under your supervision, like I do?"

> A LITTLE ENCOURAGEMENT and support here and there, even if it is inconsistent, is better than none at all.

After getting clarification on their situation (and often challenging the wisdom of the reporting structure!), I share the approach we have found to be practical and reasonably successful.

No supervisor (unless they have special powers like Superman or Wonder Woman) can successfully and genuinely keep in touch with fifty employees where they are able to know what the employee does, give them adequate oversight, instruction, and training, and get to know the employees at a personal level, and give them regular feedback and appreciation in the way each employee prefers. Not possible.

Therefore, an approach of "divide and conquer" and prioritization has to be employed. Since a supervisor cannot effectively and regularly communicate appreciation to a large number of supervisees, then smaller groups of employees have to be identified and start with them. But who?

I want to refer back to the research that found 79 percent of employees who voluntarily leave their jobs say that a key reason for their leaving is that they don't feel appreciated.[2] This means that *if your key team members don't feel truly valued, you are at risk of losing them.*

The implication? If you have a large team, you may want to identify those *key employees* so critical to your organization that, if you lost them, serious problems would follow—and focus your initial time and attention on communicating authentic appreciation to them. This approach is similar to a strengths-based approach to training individuals. You don't want to lose the strongest team members that help make your team successful.

A second group of employees to consider high priority in communicating appreciation are *those who seem to be discouraged.* After solidifying your key employees, then take more of a triage approach—look for those who need support and encouragement so they don't "check out" and become totally ineffective. This might include someone who has been working hard on a long term project and has encountered numerous obstacles making the task especially hard or delaying its progress. Come alongside of these individuals and give them encouragement—calling attention to the positive steps they have taken and give them the vision and hope of success.

The third group of employees you should focus on are those whom I described as *easy wins.* These are the people you work with on a day-to-day basis, you have a pretty good relationship with, and it would be easy for you to share your appreciation for what they do and who they are (and you can find out how they desire to be appreciated). This group gives a good "Return On Investment" for the time and energy expended. They are relatively easy to communicate appreciation to, you are likely to hit the mark with them (since you know them fairly well), and since you work closely with them, you will probably experience some of the positive results (cheerful mood, more energized, less complaining).

The final tactic is to *delegate.* If you do not have formal "team leaders" (or a similar title) that you can ask to take formal responsibility for supporting and encouraging those under their leadership, then look for those employees who are leaders by their performance, character, and behavior. Ask them for their assistance in communicating appreciation among their colleagues. Consider identifying specific employees they will focus upon in the coming weeks (two to four co-workers is a reasonable number).

While there are no simple solutions to the challenge of supervising and showing appreciation to a large number of employees, we have found this approach gets the ball rolling and has positive effects within the work group. The alternative is to feel overwhelmed and do nothing—which doesn't lead to the results the supervisor and team members want.

BEYOND BUSYNESS

Yes, people are busy. And virtually no one is looking for more work to do. But busyness and hyperactivity do not necessarily lead to a thriving workplace—they can actually be counterproductive to the health of the organization and its employees by stealing the resources needed to accomplish more important tasks.

By helping groups learn how to show appreciation to others in the specific ways meaningful to each person (rather than using a "same thing for everyone" approach) along with spreading the responsibility for communicating appreciation to coworkers, supervisors, and direct reports—then the resources of the organization, and its individual members, can be used to nourish and create a healthy work environment.

REFLECTION QUESTIONS

When you hear that busyness is the #1 reason reported why appreciation in the workplace is not communicated more, is that consistent with your perception?

What contributes to the level of busyness at your workplace?

When you hear the goal of implementing appreciation at work by slightly changing what you are already doing, what reactions do you have?

Does it make sense to you to try to communicate to employees in the ways meaningful to them versus doing the same actions for everyone? What challenges do you see associated with doing so?

How much difference do you think it will make to supervisors and managers when they learn communicating appreciation to employees is not solely *their* responsibility?

What impact do you think will occur in work groups if colleagues begin to communicate appreciation for one another (versus expecting it solely from their supervisor)?

Do you think it is realistic for coworkers to communicate appreciation when their manager isn't doing so? What do you think would happen if colleagues communicate appreciation but the supervisor doesn't?

Have you ever worked in an organization where the staff was totally overwhelmed and just trying to survive? Do you think appreciation can be communicated in this environment? Why or why not?

What ideas do you have in response to the challenges of trying to communicate appreciation to a large number of direct reports?

When you look at the list of possible groups of employees to start with, which group(s) seem most relevant to your situation?

☐ Key employees

☐ Colleagues who are discouraged

☐ "Easy wins" (people you work most directly with)

Section 3

THE CHALLENGES
OF DIFFERENCES

Differences—among individuals, across types of work settings, between cultures—are a third source of obstacles for appreciation to be effectively shown. Section 3 looks at these challenges:

- Chapter 6: the unique characteristics of various types of work settings,
- Chapter 7: the foundational differences among individuals,
- Chapter 8: the ways that cultures (both within countries and among nations) view and approach appreciation differently.

6

UNIQUE SETTINGS

Alexandra ran into Stefanie as both were filling out nametags at a YPO (Young Presidents Organization) event. "Hey, Stef, good to see you. This should be fun!" said Alex, a supervisor for a nonprofit organization that serves children and families.

"Yes, and thought provoking," added Stefanie, an assistant middle-school principal. "It's a great idea, getting lots of different types of organizations together. I'll be interested to see how all these different organizations can use this information."

The two women had signed up for a community-wide training event on "Applying the 5 languages of appreciation to Your Workplace." The event was well attended, with registration exceeding expectations—in fact, the attendance was the largest of any other training in the past several years.

Leaders from a wide range of companies and organizations were in attendance, including financial advisors and insurance firms, owners of a chain of retail lumberyards, law firms, leaders from the local hospital, managers from the city and county, the assistant superintendent and principals from the largest school district in the area, the management teams from small manufacturing firms, a regional restaurant chain, as well as not-for-profit organizations like Alex's.

The training was structured in a way that included some lecture sessions, small group discussions, video examples, large group Q&A, and personal worksheets for applying the concepts. Leaders were encouraged to mix it up and not sit with the colleagues from their firms. As a result, individuals from a variety of businesses interacted at each table.

During one of the small group discussions where the attendees were brainstorming on the practical challenges they saw of trying to apply the 5 languages of appreciation to their workshop, a stirring interchange occurred between the leaders at one table.

Mark, a division manager for the county, raised his concern: "I really like the concepts we've been discussing and I think they would be helpful to improve morale within our department. But I'm concerned about the overall sense of negativity and powerlessness frontline staff feel. I'm just not sure if working on appreciation would be able to break through that barrier."

"I agree, Mark," Margo chimed in. "Working toward communicating authentic appreciation would be really helpful at the hospital, especially among the clinical staff. But we have so much cynicism from prior trainings, things like 'write a thank-you note once a week,' that the resistance is high. And I'm not sure how we would implement 'quality time'—our staff just don't have any spare time when they are serving patients."

Stefanie, the assistant school principal, added, "We have different challenges within the schools. On the one hand, we've had a good reception to the 5 languages, since many of the teachers are familiar with *The 5 Love Languages®.* One issue we have is the fact that teachers rarely see each other teach, so that creates some difficulties in knowing what to compliment for. Also, we have a division between faculty and support staff—sort of like two groups within the school."

"Well, since we are raising concerns, I'll add mine," Jim, from the regional office of a large restaurant chain, said. "We have supervisors who oversee thirty-five to forty employees—and on two different shifts. I'm not sure how they can apply these concepts with so many people who report to them."

Alex commented, "The difficulty we have to figure out is in the language of tangible gifts. It is sort of weird thinking about giving a colleague a twenty-dollar gift card when you are working with homeless families. I hope they have some ideas for gifts that don't cost much money."

"Well, we'll see," Jim concluded, as the group was called back to the larger discussion.

INTRODUCTORY NOTE: This is a long chapter because the challenges found in numerous work settings are addressed. Rather than read the whole chapter, we recommend reading the introduction, the section on the Motivating by Appreciation Inventory, and the conclusion. Then, you can pick and choose the other sections that most directly relate to you. The work setting sections include:

- Government agencies
- Long-distance and individual work relationships
- Medical settings
- Military work settings
- Not-for-profit organizations and ministries
- Sales and sales managers
- Schools (K–12)

VIBRANT WORKPLACES: NOT ALL THE SAME

Vibrant workplaces don't all look the same. Just like a healthy tomato plant is significantly different from a thriving, growing juniper shrub, so work environments that are characterized by a positive, dynamic energy differ in many ways as well.

Shortly after releasing *The 5 Languages of Appreciation in the Workplace*, I began speaking to various groups about communicating appreciation at work effectively. As I spoke in hospital settings, businesses, the military, schools, ministries, and government agencies, I could see there were a variety of work environments with diverse needs.

I can state unequivocally that *we have yet to find a work setting in which the 5 languages of appreciation*

WE HAVE YET TO FIND a work setting in which the 5 languages of appreciation *cannot* be applied successfully.

cannot *be applied successfully.* In fact, one of the strengths of our process is that communicating authentic appreciation uses foundational principles applicable in every type of workplace, but which can be adapted for the unique aspects of each work setting.

In this chapter, we will give examples from a variety of work settings and identify the challenges often experienced. We will suggest ways to overcome those barriers, so appreciation can be successfully communicated and staff can build vibrant work settings.

THE IMPORTANCE OF THE
MOTIVATING BY APPRECIATION INVENTORY

A key step in the process of applying appreciation to various types of organizations is explaining the Motivating by Appreciation Inventory and how it works. The MBA Inventory not only identifies an individual's preferred languages of appreciation, but also the specific actions that are meaningful to them.

It is evident that unique characteristics exist in a variety of work settings, which changes what the languages of appreciation may look like in daily life. For example, an act of service in a school setting may involve watching another teacher's students so they can make some calls to parents. But in a medical setting, an act of service could be covering your colleague's patient call lights so they can get caught up on charting.

As a result, we have created a number of versions of the Motivating by Appreciation Inventory to address the specific characteristics of different work settings. These work settings include long-distance, government agencies, medical settings, the military, not-for-profits and ministries, sales and sales managers, and schools.

SPECIFIC CHALLENGES: WHAT THEY SAID

We interviewed a number of individuals in a variety of work settings to gain their thoughts about the specific challenges of communicating appreciation in their workplace, and ways to overcome the obstacles. The following answers are compiled from individuals who work in each of the settings identified and are familiar with our Appreciation at Work resources. Their responses reflect their own personal perspective and communication styles. I am thankful for their insights into how to practically apply the Appreciation at Work concepts to their unique settings.

Government agencies
• **What are the characteristics of the job/work setting that make communicating appreciation in government settings challenging?**

How promotions are given is often discouraging. The practice is to promote someone to the next grade level when they have been on the job for a certain time length, with the promotion being based solely on the time frame rather than the ability to do the job at the next level. This approach puts people at levels where they are not capable of performing at the grade level they possess. Then, as a supervisor, it becomes difficult to appreciate an employee who is not performing at the level required for the position they have.

• **What are typical assumptions or stereotypes about government employees and how they are motivated?**

The typical stereotype of government employees is that they are lazy and bad workers. While there are some in the system matching that stereotype, it is not the norm. There are a lot of hard workers in government service who care about the job they do and take great pride in doing a good job.

• **What are common negative reactions to appreciation—either from frontline employees, their supervisors or higher-level management?**

I think common negative reactions that come from frontline employees are, "It's good enough for government work" or "No one cares anyway." So often they don't seem motivated to do quality work, which makes it hard to appreciate them for what they do.

Then supervisors develop an attitude of "If you want something done right, you have to do it yourself." A lack of confidence in staff grows and expands into the higher-level administrators. This obviously doesn't lead to a sense of trust in others or feeling pride about what you are doing as a unit.

Add to these dynamics the seemingly constant change (leadership, rules, procedures, priorities) that occurs within organizations, and you have a growing cynicism and negativity across all levels—because they don't have much hope that true change will ever happen.

• **What are some guiding principles for implementing appreciation within government settings?**

The main guiding principle in a government setting is that change has to happen from the top. Employees will follow an example set by upper management. While some employees at lower levels may be motivated to change, support and leadership from supervisors and managers needs to happen in order for the changes to really stick.

©Glasbergen
glasbergen.com

"How do you feel about letting your people work from home?"

• **Are there pitfalls or mistakes to avoid?**

The biggest pitfall is the lack of follow-through that seems to occur repeatedly.

• **Are there some positive action steps or approaches to take that will help overcome the common challenges?**

One of the steps that has helped thus far is to create teams. Get the people who are motivated together to help keep deadlines and goals on target. Working together to apply the concept of authentic appreciation and learning from one another's experiences with your groups is really helpful to stay on track and keep going.

LONG-DISTANCE/VIRTUAL

• **What are the characteristics of the work in a long-distance work relationship or virtual work setting that make communicating appreciation challenging?**

The most obvious hurdle is the limited face-to-face communication with your coworkers. Most of the interaction is by phone and email, with occasional video conferences. This is "the nature of the beast"—

and for some employees is more of an issue than for others.

Working off-site (or in a totally virtual work group) provides fewer day-to-day opportunities to get to know your coworkers professionally and personally. Fewer spontaneous interactions occur, whether it is just asking about a colleague's weekend or getting together on the spur of the moment to discuss an issue with the team.

Because of this, fewer interactions and opportunities exist to build relationships and trust. Relationships can be "strictly business," where all interactions are just about the tasks that need to be completed.

For the virtual employee trying to communicate appreciation to other team members, expressing your thoughts in writing can sometimes be more difficult than just a casual verbal comment.

• **What are typical assumptions or stereotypes about virtual or long distance employees and how they are motivated?**

Virtual employees typically value time flexibility (scheduling their workday when it fits their schedule and prime work hours), and also being able to work in various places that support the ways they work best.

Successful off-site employees (not everyone does well in these types of work settings) are able to work with less day-to-day supervision. They tend to be motivated more by results (getting tasks done) and often are entrepreneurial, being motivated by sales made and revenue generated.

WHEN YOU WORK OFF-SITE, there can be a sense of others not truly understanding what you do.

One important aspect of working off-site is that one's peers or supervisor don't see all that you are doing, and may not realize all the time and effort it took to complete a task or reach the goal obtained. So there can be a sense of others not truly understanding what you do.

• **What are common negative reactions to appreciation—either from virtual employees, their supervisors, or management?**

Since there is generally less interaction, the nature of the relationship with colleagues and supervisor is different. The interactions tend to be more businesslike (factual, about tasks), and a less emotional, caring relationship can develop. This can then make it difficult (for both parties) to communicate appreciation to one another—because it crosses over into the emotional/relational realm.

Eventually, some employees can feel totally disconnected from the rest of their work group, and feel treated just like a "work unit" because virtually all of their interactions are about task completion.

• **What are some guiding principles for implementing appreciation within long distance work relationships?**

There seems to be two major components: *structured time* and *spontaneous interactions*. In some situations, if time for interacting is not structured, it will rarely happen. This includes phone calls, video-conferences, and occasional face-to-face times. When these occur, it is important to use the opportunity wisely to build the relationship beyond just work tasks. Involving off-site employees in team celebrations (even if it is virtual via video) is important, rather than just leaving them out. Sometimes it is important to let the employee choose whether they want to take the time and effort to come to an event: while you may think it is too much to ask, they feel honored to be invited and included.

When possible, create other types of activities that can be done together to build your relationship—going to meals together or doing a fun activity together after a meeting.

Since building trust is more difficult in virtual work relationships, keeping your word and acting with integrity is huge. This includes being on time and showing up for scheduled calls or videoconferences. Following through on a commitment made to get a resource for the team member, or setting up a meeting with another leader who can help them more easily get a task done, helps them feel like they are important to you.

Since spontaneous interactions (walking in from the parking lot, seeing each other in the hallway) are infrequent, you almost have to "schedule" nonscheduled conversations. Set up a time to talk (by phone or video) just to catch up, or leave some time to chat before or after a scheduled conference call.

Be proactive in talking to the team member about non-work issues: What's going on with their family? What did they do over the weekend? Ask about any non-work projects (e.g., remodeling, moving) they are involved in, or talk about local sporting events.

Give your virtual employees the opportunity to share what would be helpful to them. Ask: "How can I help you?" Listen, and then do what you can to help make their request happen.

• **Are there pitfalls or mistakes to avoid?**

The key one that comes to mind is a lack of follow-up. If you say, "I'll get back to you by the end of the week" but don't (because not seeing them doesn't remind you), that sends the message that the employee isn't important to you.

• **Are there some positive action steps or approaches to take that will help overcome the common challenges?**

Consistently work to build trust and communication. This can't be overemphasized in long distance work relationships.

MEDICAL SETTINGS

• **What characteristics of the job/work settings make communicating appreciation in a healthcare setting challenging?**

TIME is huge. It seems like we are always behind in our work and it feels like there's never enough time to do all we are supposed to. So having ways to communicate appreciation quickly and easily, on an ongoing daily basis, is needed.

All healthcare providers live under the tyranny of the urgent—but this tyranny is different in healthcare because people's lives depend on our timeliness. As a result, we feel extra pressure. The lack of time available makes it important to find brief but meaningful ways of communicating appreciation.

For nurse managers, this can include making rounds on the floor in between meetings and checking in with staff. If a nurse is with a patient, waiting for them to finish their task (versus interrupting or just passing by) can send a message.

Coming in to check with night shift staff can be really impactful (nightshift workers often feel like the "stepchild"). Even if they are not available, leaving them a note with your phone number and inviting them to call you can be encouraging.

Arrogance seems to be a prevalent issue. There is clearly the attitude among some: "Why do you need to appreciate people for doing their job? I do mine. Why don't you just do yours?"

Another challenge is the difficulty of balancing the need for constructive feedback (especially in a training setting) versus appreciation. Sometimes staff have difficulty accepting that they can be appreciated and valued, but at the same time have areas in which they need to improve.

• **What are some typical assumptions or stereotypes about nurses, staff, managers, and how they are motivated?**

Some people outside of the healthcare system seem to believe that healthcare professionals (especially doctors or specialists) mainly do what they do for the money. That doesn't seem to be true for most healthcare professionals—the work is not primarily about money. It is about caring for the patient.

Another negative stereotype is when people think we just come to do our shift, and that's it. It's possible some clinical staff are like that, but the great majority are not. We are most motivated when we do something that makes a difference, not necessarily that our boss or other people or even the patient knows. It's that WE know we made a difference.

Regarding tangible rewards, nurses and support staff don't need big things—it's the little things from management that can make a difference. For example, when a local hospital took away the staff's meal discount benefit (it wasn't much, but it was something), morale went down. It's not clear how much this discount was costing the hospital but everyone felt betrayed; the staff all decided we'd never purchase hospital cafeteria food again. Later, the hospital significantly reduced our shift differentials—that is, the extra amount paid for working evenings, nights, or weekends. That saved the hospital a lot of money, but again, we felt insignificant and not important.

Similarly, make sure that if some special treats are provided for the unit that there is enough food for everyone. It is really discouraging as a clinician serving patients to finish up with your patients at the end of your shift, go to get a snack, and all the food is gone.

• **What are common types of reactions (negative, resistant) to an appreciation approach—either from the frontline staff themselves or supervisors and managers?**

Given that medical settings are usually focused on problems, healthcare professionals tend to look for the "negative" and then try to problem-solve. "What's wrong here? Why isn't this working better?" As a result, the negatives stand out more in people's minds, and they have difficulty thinking of positive things to appreciate each other for.

Sometimes people wonder how much thought went into the appreciation given—is it sincere? Or is the person being manipulative? Appreciation needs to be consistent and regular. If it is communicated only sporadically, then the motives for appreciation become suspect.

- **What guiding principles would you give for working well with healthcare staff, pitfalls/mistakes to avoid?**

Appreciation seems to be the most meaningful when it is communicated in a timely fashion, and when frontline staff hear positive comments from the professionals. Healthcare professionals need to become more aware of the potential positive impact they can have on their team members' morale with just a little effort.

Appreciation *Can* Work in Medical Settings

One outpatient physical therapy clinic had their staff take the *MBA Inventory* and began to practice communicating appreciation in each person's primary language—and even just tried to increase saying "thanks" to one another more regularly. After working with them periodically over four months, they said to me, "Dr. Paul, we don't need you anymore. Appreciation has become part of our culture now!"

- **Are there positive action steps/approaches to take that will help overcome these common challenges?**

Be committed to implementing appreciation in the workplace over time. Make sure staff know it is not just another "flavor of the month" flash. Incorporate the process of showing appreciation in team meetings, and have follow-up training and discussions.

Being willing to help when a colleague is feeling overwhelmed is huge. Once, a nurse manager came in with her scrubs on (versus office clothing) and said, "How can I help?" It was encouraging to see that she was willing to get her hands dirty and help out practically.

Again, don't underestimate the impact of food as an act of encouragement can be an encouragement. When you work twelve-hour shifts, some muffins or some snacks on a cart can be a real boost, both physically and emotionally!

MILITARY SETTINGS

• **What are the characteristics of the job/work setting that make communicating appreciation in the military challenging?**

Communicating appreciation in a military setting can be especially difficult due to two issues: a) the overall military culture, and b) the systems of reward and recognition already in place.

The military culture (speaking in generalities here) is very focused on achievement and perception. There are specific and public goals to achieve (being promoted, completing a school, being assigned to a special unit) that have outward symbols of achievement (rank insignia, badges, unit and deployment patches). These achievements all have very clearly defined "rules" for achieving them.

There are also well-defined systems of reward, some of which are more public than others. For instance, being awarded a medal often comes with an outward display of recognition, such as a ceremony with a physical medal or ribbon.

It is important to note that a significant challenge in military settings is differentiating between recognition for achievement and appreciation for the individual. Since performance recognition is a core aspect of the culture, many times supervisors and officers need extra help in seeing how appreciation for the individual at a personal level can complement achievement awards. A simple example should suffice: it is not uncommon for leaders to receive an order that achievement awards should be determined for the unit. Sometimes an officer or supervisor may then direct the unit members to write up their own report recommending (themselves) for an achievement award—which doesn't really engender a sense of authentic appreciation by the recipient!

• **What are typical assumptions or stereotypes about servicemen and women and how they are motivated?**

A typical stereotype about servicemen and women is that they are only outwardly goal-oriented in both their motivation and their preference for receiving appreciation. In one sense, virtually all military personnel are concerned with the outward displays of appreciation that the military highlights. This is because, in very real terms, their livelihood is determined by how they are assessed in their performance reports, by what medals and badges they have received, and with which units they have served (for example, the 101st Airborne Division). This emphasis on external recognition does not mean, however, that those performance awards are *all* that is important to service members. Just as much as any other individual, service members may desire to receive personal, authentic appreciation communicated in the ways they value.

• **What are common negative reactions to an appreciation approach—either from enlisted personnel themselves, their supervisors or officers?**

A service member may feel resistant to certain forms of appreciation that could be viewed as soft or touchy-feely. The military system values results, and the rewards system is built to prize behavior that gets results. Thus, anything that does not specifically lead to an observable result may be seen as unnecessary and be discarded. Words, for instance, are seen as helpful tools for encouraging specific behavior and discouraging other behavior. But the use of words in an excessive or unnecessary manner that does not specifically lead to mission accomplishment (such as encouragement) could easily be jettisoned in lieu of a use of time and energy that immediately gets results.

A common sarcastic remark one might hear in response to the suggestion of improving communicating appreciation might be: "If the Army wanted you to have an appreciation language, it would have issued you one!" That is, the Army knows best and will give you everything (and only) what you need.

On the other hand, the military system *does* value physical touch and camaraderie in a way that much of the rest of the culture does not.

• **What are some guiding principles for implementing appreciation with military personnel?**

Leaders must get out of the mindset that you only do the types of appreciation that are within the confines of the military system. People really want to know that you care for them, not that what you are doing for them is done just "because that is what we do."

• **Are there pitfalls or mistakes to avoid?**

Sometimes *not* giving an award/promotion/evaluation that is due to an individual can be more damaging than any amount of other appreciation. This is especially the case in the military, where these types of appreciation have very outward displays and significant career implications.

• **Are there some positive action steps or approaches to take that will help overcome the common challenges?**

Showing genuine care and concern is most important. Two important keys:

Realize that there are other ways to genuinely show appreciation outside of the military system of awards, badges, and pins (be creative!).

Remember that any appreciation should be done genuinely (and that what is not done also speaks volumes).

**Please see how to obtain the article "Resiliency, Social Support & Appreciation in the Workplace" in the Free eBook and Additional Resources section in the back of the book.

NOT-FOR-PROFITS (NFPS)/MINISTRIES

• **What are some guiding principles for implementing appreciation within nonprofit organizations?**

Start with the main leadership staff and then focus on the key volunteer leaders, particularly those who lead many volunteers. From the nonprofits I have worked with, learning to look for the character and personal qualities their fellow staff and volunteers bring to the table (in addition to what they do) has been the "aha" moment in the Appreciation at Work training.

• **Are there pitfalls or mistakes to avoid?**

In an effort to be fair when giving small tangible gifts, don't just give the same gift! Get creative and learn about the individual—what they enjoy, sports, hobbies, etc. This can be a huge win for making others feel individually noticed and appreciated when you can take the time to learn about the staff or volunteer.

Many staff teams work long hours and give tirelessly to their organization's mission, serving volunteers and clients. The staff often has little time to appreciate each other and can easily take one another for granted. A team-building event or retreat using the Appreciation at Work materials is clearly a valuable culture enhancer!

• **Are there some positive action steps or approaches to take that will help overcome the common challenges?**

Change things up! Instead of the appreciation picnic, lunch or dinner, take the time to learn and connect with volunteers, particularly key ones in leadership roles.

For the staff, planning and hosting appreciation events takes a ton of time and effort. If, over time, putting on these big events was replaced with more individual appreciation, it would be better received by the staff and the volunteer recipients, and could take less time as well!

SALES/SALES MANAGEMENT

NOTE: While "sales" and "sales management" is not a specific industry by itself (they occur within most for-profit companies), the characteristics of sales teams are sufficiently different from other roles in companies that we felt it was important to address their challenges separately.

• **What are the characteristics of the job/work setting that make communicating appreciation to salespersons challenging?**

The emphasis on sales by management and business leaders is huge. They truly function on the belief that "nothing gets done until something gets sold." As a result, there is a high degree of performance recognition built into sales organizations because results are vitally important to the business and easily measured (booked sales, revenue, gross profit, etc.).

The focus on performance for sales personnel is reflected by these common practices:

• Results are usually posted publicly, highlighting the top performers.
• Many sales positions have a variable pay component (bonuses and commissions) that directly rewards higher performance.
• Historically, much of the sales coaching has solely focused on results, with little feedback or reinforcement on the behaviors and character traits that lead to those results.
• Celebration, be it formal or casual, is usually expressed by/with the salesperson almost exclusively when a sale is made.
• The net impact of continual recognition and feedback being focused solely on results gives the illusion that sufficient "appreciation" is being conveyed, and no other actions are needed.

Thus, the expression of the individual's value (apart from performance) is discounted or dismissed.

• **What are typical assumptions or stereotypes about sales personnel and how they are motivated?**

Sales positions tend to be some of the most financially rewarding positions. People with high financial aspirations gravitate towards sales positions. Focusing on the money-only view of sales and assuming that the ONLY motivation of a salesperson is money leads to a distorted view of salespeople. Conversely, the positive character-based behaviors leading toward a trusting relationship need to be valued for the good of the salesperson and the business.

• **What are common negative reactions to an appreciation approach—either from salespeople themselves or sales managers?**

One of the most frequent responses by sales executives (those who oversee the sales team) is "Their appreciation is in their commission check." Supervisors and managers in other areas of the business sometimes comment, "Sales reps are coin-operated." These types of responses stem from belief that financial rewards are the primary (if not sole) motivator for those who work in sales.

Similarly, many sales managers fear that an appreciation message to their team members may be taken as a license to produce less. "If I say to Jim, 'You're doing a good job in finding new customers,' he may take his foot off the pedal a bit, and slow down—which is the exact opposite of what I want to happen."

Salespeople must maintain a positive attitude to face rejection daily. It may appear to those around them (especially non-sales colleagues) that they are doing great and are super-encouraged. As a result, the projection of this upbeat attitude may cause others to withhold appreciation because they feel there is no need for it.

For the salespersons themselves, a cynical attitude may be their first response to a message of appreciation: "That's nice, but what do you really want from me?" Or, "Okay, since I'm so good, how much are you going to raise my quota?" This reflects their belief (or prior experience) that the primary purpose of a compliment is to "set up" the salesperson to agree to a new or increased demand.

• **What are some guiding principles for implementing appreciation with sales personnel? Are there pitfalls or mistakes to avoid?**

For sales personnel, while they value appreciation expressed by their manager or colleagues, any appreciation communicated by a customer carries a very high value. Essentially, the customer is an "amplification factor"—any appreciation expressed that includes positive feedback from the customer will be hugely impactful on the salesperson.

Conversely, a strong sense of disrespect will result if any action hinders a customer relationship. One rep said, "I have a new manager who makes me feel insignificant by not responding to my email and texts in a timely fashion, making it difficult for me to get customers their quotes."

Any expression of appreciation regarding the salesperson's character can have a significant impact. Because the sales process is so strongly focused on the ultimate result of a sale, sales personnel become weary of recognition directed to performance-producing behaviors. Therefore, calling attention to other character qualities can deeply resonate with sales personnel. For example, a salesperson shared, "When a team member expressed how much he valued my opinion in how to handle a sales situation he was encountering, I was humbled!"

FOR SALES PERSONNEL, any appreciation communicated by a customer carries a high value.

Don't wait until the sale is booked to communicate appreciation. Sales positions tend to require high amounts of personal courage and risk-taking to demonstrate the right behaviors for prospecting, qualifying, calling on executives, and dealing with customer satisfaction issues. Expressing appreciation to a sales rep who displays positive character qualities and success-oriented behavior is critical, even when immediate business results are not yet visible.

• **Are there some positive action steps or approaches to take that will help overcome the common challenges?**

Non-sales team members should express appreciation to salespersons. One salesperson reported she received a handwritten note of "job well done" with the statement at the end of the note: "I can always depend on you." She said, "Receiving a note like that pumps you up and sets a subtle expectation at the same time. It was a low-pressure /high-yield message of thanks for doing your job and going beyond expectations."

SCHOOLS

• **What are the characteristics of working in a school setting that make communicating appreciation to faculty and staff challenging?**

When you have only one thirty-minute staff meeting a month (typically before school), it makes building relationships challenging because there's so little time for anything "extra." With the short planning period that each teacher has at a different time, a person would really have to plan ahead to do anything specific for another on staff.

For administrators and principals, a challenge is to know what a teacher really does in the classroom. An administrator can occasionally spend five or ten minutes in a classroom, but that only gives a glimpse of what goes on. Teachers rarely see what another teacher does during a class, so there is not a lot of data on which to base appreciation for colleagues.

Teachers in public schools often feel defensive because they feel our society does not see teachers as professionals but as "public servant people." This leads school professionals to feel like they have to prove themselves and therefore, they can be reluctant to receive praise. This posture also can create a sense of competitiveness and becomes counterproductive to teamwork and collaboration.

Another practical aspect of school settings that creates ongoing challenges is the fact that school personnel are frequently moved from building to building. As a result, team members may just be getting to know one another and how to support and encourage each other when one of them is transferred to another school. (This is especially difficult for administrators who have multiple staff to get to know.)

• **What are typical assumptions or stereotypes about faculty and staff, and how they are motivated?**

Many administrators and principals believe a general email saying "good job" is enough to encourage a staff member, seemingly because that's the easiest action to take, even though it is not personal or meaningful.

Those who are not teachers (especially parents and administrators) assume that a class's test scores make an educator feel like they are a good teacher. In reality, many teachers know that the test data does not define them as a teacher any more than the scores define the kids.

Food is actually a pretty good motivator, and it takes many shapes and forms:

• The PTO providing snacks or a meal during parent/teacher conferences.
• The principal buying dinner before an evening open house.
• A random snack with a note left in your mailbox or on the desk.

While the actions are usually well intended, don't assume that free food makes teachers feel appreciated—that's not always the case.

126

While a workroom full of food often becomes a gathering place, many teachers would rather be home with their families . . . and also eating healthier meals.

MANY TEACHERS KNOW THAT the test data does not define them as a teacher any more than the scores define the kids.

One of the assumptions that teachers and school personnel most resent is: "Teachers don't need motivation because they only work from eight to four and they get summers off." In contrast, during the school year, teachers feel supported when they are given extra planning periods or workdays without students, not only to allow for preparation but also for more time to collaborate with other staff.

• **What are common negative reactions to an appreciation approach—either from faculty and staff themselves or principals and administrators?**

When a program (like a meeting about recordkeeping or safety issues) is scheduled, it throws everything out of balance and sometimes makes us feel like our jobs are not as important. These meetings are important, but they take away from what we need to do for the kids. So when a "we appreciate you" program is required, it has the same negative resistance. "Thanks, but no thanks!"

• **When have you seen appreciation start to make a difference?**

Appreciation makes a difference when it is personal, deserved, and meaningful.

I think sometimes appreciation is more about the climate of the building than the act itself. The way the leadership (principals, counselors, administrators) communicates on a regular basis makes the faculty and staff feel respected and professional. A positive tone and cheerful demeanor when communicating with staff goes a long way to laying a foundation for a healthy work environment.

• **What are some guiding principles for implementing appreciation with school personnel?**

Understand that teachers do not clock out after the last bell. They work with kids after school and most take work home every night, as well as spending several hours on the weekend grading and preparing. It's absolutely crucial to recognize that every teacher works extremely hard, because it's a calling, a love for the profession of teaching. Understanding this makes all the difference when it comes to communicating appreciation.

• **Are there pitfalls or mistakes to avoid?**

"Fairness" seems to be a big issue within schools. Teachers and staff are quite sensitive (probably overly so) to "who gets what" and whether another teacher is getting more of the assistant principal's time than they are, or if one team member seems to win prizes more than would seem random at celebrations. Be aware of gossip and pockets of grumbling; try to address the concerns directly and as quickly as possible.

• **Are there some positive action steps or approaches to take that will help overcome the common challenges?**

Give the staff a chance to get to know each other. With everyone being so busy and focused on their own personal classroom and students, it is not uncommon for teachers to rarely see each other, especially when they have different planning periods and lunchtimes.

CONCLUSION:
WORKING *WITH* YOUR ORGANIZATION'S STRUCTURE

Work settings differ significantly, creating both windows of opportunity and potential barriers for applying the 5 languages of appreciation. But we have found that by making a few "tweaks" and working *with* the structure of the organization, authentic appreciation can become a vital part of any organizational culture and help create a healthy, vibrant workplace.

There are obviously numerous other industries and types of work settings that have their own particular challenges. We are not able to discuss all of them here. But, hopefully, the lessons learned from the previous examples will give some insight into how to approach some of the challenges encountered in alternate work settings.

REFLECTION QUESTIONS

When you think about the variety of work settings in which you have worked, which ones were difficult for communicating authentic appreciation? Why was this the case?

From the expanded list below, identify the three work settings that you think provide the most challenges to communicating appreciation to employees. Share why you think they would be difficult settings.

☐ Retail	☐ Restaurants and hotels
☐ Manufacturing	☐ Telecommunications
☐ IT	☐ Construction
☐ Utilities	☐ Oil and gas
☐ Small family businesses	☐ Law enforcement
	☐ Large corporations
☐ Other _____	☐ Other _____

In which of the above work settings do you think authentic appreciation is the most needed? Why?

1.

2.

3.

What specific challenges do you think there might be in communicating appreciation in work relationships across long distances?

Consider the work settings discussed in the chapter. Pick one setting from the list below and share ideas you have that could help in communicating appreciation in that setting.

☐ Schools (K–12)

☐ Medical settings/hospitals

☐ Military

☐ Nonprofit organizations

☐ Ministries

☐ Sales/sales management

☐ Government

7

PEOPLE ARE DIFFERENT—BUT WE TREAT THEM THE SAME

H ey, Simon," said John as he poured himself his first cup of coffee of the morning. Simon greeted him, filled up his big water bottle, and went in to his workstation to start his day in customer service. John gazed after him thoughtfully. He liked Simon, who had been with the company about a year. But, he had to admit to himself, he was beginning to lose patience with the young man—one of his direct reports.

What was the problem? Simon was bright enough, personable, and capable in relating to upset customers. He got along with his co-workers. But, John thought, Simon was careless. He did a terrible job filling out the paperwork to document his customer interactions. He tended to show up ten or fifteen minutes late to work, even after John had spoken to him about it a couple of times. Sometimes he was late coming back from lunch. John, in his forties and a veteran of the company, believed these things mattered.

And there was more, as John vented to his wife that evening. "He's always either on his phone texting, or he's checking out websites for information he's interested in—not work-related. I've talked to him, and he always nods and says 'Okay,' but nothing really changes. The problem is, he meets the standards set by the company and he gets high ratings from the customers, so there's really nothing I can do. Even if I send him an email or text, thanking him for something positive I've observed in his work, he doesn't respond. It's like the messages go into a black hole. Only when I ask him directly, 'Did you get my email about that difficult client?' will he say, 'Yeah. Got it. Thanks.'

"We all took that inventory I told you about, with the appreciation languages, and I know from that his language is Quality Time, but all of the actions he chose were about spending time with his peers, going out after work or watching sports together. But there weren't any actions that included me. I'm just not sure what I'm supposed to do."

If you haven't noticed, the world is composed of things different from one another. Not only different objects (rocks, water, clouds, plants), but each type of object varies widely as well. Sandstone, granite, gypsum, marble are all varieties of rock. Eagles, hummingbirds, cardinals are all species of birds.

One of the most fascinating patterns in nature is the aspect of variation within similar organisms. All trees have roots, trunks, limbs, and leaves; but the variation across species (oak, palm, fir) as well as among the individual trees is virtually mind-blowing. All dogs have four legs, a tail, and love eating food, but a poodle is not like a Lab. And, as any dog owner can attest, you will find personality differences even within the various breeds. But all these differences are needed for a healthy, vibrant ecosystem.

Similarly, people differ in so many ways—shapes, sizes, age, abilities, family history, personal life experiences, educational background, ways of thinking, personality style, values—the list seems almost endless. Siblings can be very different from each other, despite sharing DNA! As the famous social scientist Margaret Mead said: "Always remember that you are absolutely unique. Just like everyone else."

If we were all the same, life would be extremely boring. The fact that each of us has so many unique aspects to our lives brings a richness and "interestingness" to life.

EVERYONE IS NOT LIKE YOU!

On the other hand, differences create challenges for us. On the surface, this seems obvious. But if you take a closer look at how you act and communicate with others, it may become evident that you actually treat everyone pretty much the same—in the ways that are most comfortable for *you*.

We may not understand where another person is coming from: how they are thinking about a situation or how they reached the conclusion they did. Or we have a hard time communicating our thoughts to others in a way that we feel understood . . . because they think, feel, and view life differently than we do.

In fact, one of the key skill sets for children to develop in order to function in life is to come to understand that not everyone thinks the same (or wants the same thing) as they do. Just because *they* want to go swimming doesn't mean that their dad does. This ability to comprehend that you are not the center of the universe (called "egocentrism" in psychological terms) varies in adults as well. That is, some adults still think it's all about them, which is reflected in their conversations primarily focusing on . . . them.

SEEING AS OTHERS SEE

Another key life skill that begins to develop in early childhood and (hopefully) continues to grow throughout one's lifetime is the ability to see a situation from another person's point of view. Called "perspective-taking ability," this skill is critical in developing relationships with others both at a personal and professional level. In the workplace, leaders and sales personnel, if they're going to be successful, have to be able to understand how others view situations.

Perspective-taking ability first requires the ability to "de-center"—to take yourself out of the center of the situation and realize that not everyone experiences or thinks about an event in the same way you do. To use an extreme example, think about an electrical short occurring in an office electrical outlet; it creates sparks, smokes, and something catches fire. The person at whose desk the fire occurs has a different experience than someone across the room, which varies again from a leader and her team who have to leave the building because the smoke alarm goes off (but they don't know why).

An individual who doesn't have very well-developed perspective-taking may focus on how inconvenient it was for her team meeting to be disrupted, while not thinking about how scary a situation that was for her friend who was in the office where the fire occurred.

Other more common work-related situations that require perspective-taking include:

- when, in an organizational restructuring, you are not laid off, but one of your colleagues is;
- understanding why a customer is choosing not to purchase your product when it is obvious to you that buying it is the best option for them;
- becoming frustrated with your team members when they are upset with you for delivering a message from management about a freeze on overtime, even though it wasn't your decision.

We hear a lot about "empathy" these days. This is a subtype of perspective-taking that relates to how others *feel* in a situation. Again, as human beings, we differ in our empathy levels. Some people are very in tune with others' feeling reactions, while some of us are almost clueless about how our actions may impact others and how they feel in response.

One level of empathy is considered *cognitive empathy*, where a person, at least at an intellectual level, is aware of how their actions have consequences and impact others. At this level, a person is aware of and can talk about others' feelings (and that they may be different from your own). Intellectually understanding that another person is hurt and anxious when they have lost their job is an example.

A second level is called *emotional empathy*. This is the ability and experience of "feeling with" someone else. A person with emotional empathy is able to experience along with others the same feeling reaction their colleague is having. Feeling sad (at a personal, experiential level) when your friend tells you that his mother just died is an example.

The third type of empathy, *compassionate empathy*, is demonstrated by those who not only "feel with" another person but are actually moved to do something for the other person to try to help. This compassionate empathy leads one to act in a way to help reduce the other person's distress—writing a note or offering to help in some practical way.[1]

Why is understanding perspective-taking and empathy important? Because if we have problems *seeing* a situation from another person's perspective, we are unable to understand them and their reactions. And practically speaking, our lack of understanding those around us creates challenges in communication, in working collaboratively, in making decisions together, and in selling our products and services to others.

"HOW WOULD I FEEL IF . . ."

Understanding our differences is a key step in being able to see and take into consideration other individuals' life history and experience as we work together. If you feel this is an area in which you need to (or want to) grow, there are some practical steps you can take. First, remember the saying, attributed to Native Americans, "To understand a man, you must walk a mile in his moccasins." While most of us can *intellectually* try to think what a situation is like from another person's perspective, actually experiencing what they experience on a day-to-day basis is when we really learn the lesson. This is actually the wisdom behind the popular television series *Undercover Boss*, where the president or CEO of a company goes and works in a frontline employee position for a week. Time and time again, you see the lights come on in the leader's eyes—gaining a true understanding of the challenges experienced by his or her employees.

The implication is: if you want to truly understand what another person is going through, go "live with" them. If you are a manager, spend a day shadowing one of your team members who installs products in people's homes, or with the floor salesperson who is trying to meet the needs of your customers while also keeping track of inventory.

After experiencing life with them, be sure and ask yourself a few questions:

- What would life be like if I did that work day in and day out?
- How would I feel if I were that employee, doing the tasks they do, earning what they earn, and then receiving the messages they get from management?
- How would I feel if I knew the circumstances in my life made it so that this is what I'm going to be doing for the next five years of my life, with no chance of advancement?

NOT EVERYONE FEELS APPRECIATED IN THE SAME WAY

One of the core concepts of our applying the 5 languages to work-based relationships is that *not everyone feels appreciated in the same ways*. So if you want to effectively hit the mark in communicating appreciation to those with whom you work, learning the ways they prefer to be shown appreciation is key.

Initially, the Motivating by Appreciation Inventory focused on identifying the languages of appreciation desired. We then discovered that the specific desired actions *within* that appreciation language vary significantly from individual to individual, as well. So for example, if an employee's preferred language is Quality Time, he might value a one-on-one conversation with his boss more than a team lunch. But his officemate in the next cubicle might love lunch with the gang! Or our introvert employee might want to go work out with a colleague during lunch but isn't interested in hanging out with a direct report. The iterations are many, and the inventory assesses them for you. Also, we are currently developing a version that will give employees the ability to identify those actions they really *don't* like, so colleagues and supervisors can avoid creating offense accidentally.

While the concept of not everyone feeling appreciated similarly may seem obvious to those familiar with the 5 languages of appreciation, the point remains important and seems to need repeating because *many, many leaders don't get it.* In fact, I had a division vice president of a large international manufacturing firm assert: "I have one language— time—and if that doesn't meet their need, I guess they're left out. Either they figure out that is my currency, both how I give and receive appreciation, or they don't get it from me."

We may not fully understand why that language or action is important to them, especially when their primary language is our least valued language. But we still need to accept the fact that Acts of Service (or whatever is their primary language) is what makes them feel valued, even though it does nothing for us.

> "I HAVE ONE LANGUAGE— time—and if that doesn't meet their need, I guess they're left out."

GENERATIONAL

Differences among generations in the workplace have become a huge focus—partly because there do seem to be true differences that are creating challenges in understanding employees from different generations. Since we as individuals are shaped by our life experiences, groups of people who have similar life experiences tend to think and respond to situations more similarly than others who didn't share those life experiences.

Think about the Greatest Generation and the impact of World War II on them; baby boomers who were raised during times of economic prosperity but also lived through rapid social change; Gen-Xers who often grew up the children of divorce and with MTV; or millennials who have only known life with social media, smartphones, and trophies for participation. The fact that individuals from these eras and life experiences are dissimilar to one another in many ways should not be a surprise.

But part of the struggle also seems to be related to the human tendency to group people together and treat them like they are all the same. (Unfortunately, this has and continues to be a pattern across history and cultures—with one group of people making inferences and generalizations about another perceived group based on ethnicity, race, cultural heritage, age, geographic location . . .)

I am not a full-fledged expert on the differences that create conflicts between generations. But I have done some research on a couple of workplace issues that relate to challenges in communicating appreciation across generations.

THE PROBLEM OF "GENERATIONALIZING"

In our culture, we sometimes use the term "generalizing," which describes the process of taking trends and information from a smaller set of data and inferring conclusions about the larger group. For example, we may make conclusions about the graduating class of 2017 by looking at a smaller number of students graduating from college in 2017, and infer the same characteristics for *all* of the graduates. This practice is common in research and generally considered acceptable as long as the following two principles are followed: a) the "sample" (smaller) group is an accurate representation of the larger population, and b) the conclusions made are general statements about the group as a whole and are not intended to be accurate for every individual. Why? Because the information is about the *group*, and there will be differences across the individuals within the group.

We can take this principle further and apply it to generations, which I call "*generationalizing.*" Groups of people (same age, from the same region, same gender) can share similar characteristics, but there are obviously individual differences within or across group members. Also, the characteristics can be true of other groups (for example, not every fifty-year-old employee is a hard worker). *While there are often trends that can be seen across groups of individuals within generations, it is dangerous to make assumptions about individuals solely from the group tendencies.*

> "I'M TIRED OF EVERYONE assuming that I'm a slacker because I'm only twenty-three."

For example, in discussing this topic with a large group of multigenerational workers, one young woman stated, "I'm tired of everyone assuming that I'm a slacker because I'm only twenty-three. It is offensive to me." And in this case it was true—she was identified as a hardworking young rising star.

GENERATIONS AND APPRECIATION

The first question that is asked repeatedly is: *Are there differences across generations with regard to how they like to be shown appreciation?*

As far as we can tell, there are no major differences across generations with regard to which languages of appreciation are preferred. We have just started gathering data on this, so we don't have a definitive answer yet. But all indicators are pointing to the conclusion that what generation you are from does not significantly affect which appreciation language you prefer.

That said, we *are* finding some differences across generations in the specific actions of appreciation they prefer and value most:

Time off. As is well known, many younger workers desire a flexible schedule and receiving time off (in some work settings, known as "comp time") as a reward for working hard to complete a project. Since in many ways time has become the most valuable resource we have (everyone feels like they don't have enough), it makes sense that free time is highly valued.

It is important to clarify, however, that in terms of the Languages of Appreciation, getting time off from work is not a type of Quality Time. Rather, getting off from work early on a Friday afternoon is a type of Tangible Gift, since it really is a benefit (a form of paid time off). The language of Quality Time refers to the desire that people have to spend time with others, and they feel valued when this happens.

Handwritten notes—or not. For those of us from an older generation, we were raised to believe that one of the highest forms of showing appreciation was to write a handwritten thank-you note. (Remember when you received a nice birthday present from your grandparents and your mother forced you to sit down and write a note?) Times have changed. For many younger workers, the value of handwritten notes has declined. This seems to be especially true for twentysomething males— receiving a handwritten note of encouragement adds *no value* to them (but true for only about 50 percent of twentysomething women).

Rather, what *is* important to younger colleagues is the speed with which they receive feedback. Immediate is great. Today is good. Tomorrow is acceptable. After that, you've moved into the realm of history. So if you want to be effective in communicating that you valued their work on a task, let them know as soon as you can.

Working collaboratively. When thinking about specific actions within the language of Quality Time, younger team members are more interested in working together with colleagues on a project than older generations are.

Baby boomers and older Gen-Xers are fine with working in teams to get tasks done, but they have more of a divide-and-conquer approach where they meet together to determine the common goal and then delegate tasks to accomplish individually. Younger employees generally enjoy the process of hanging out together to work cooperatively to achieve the final product.

"I could be a more effective member of the team if the others would just shut up and go away."

Recognizing team accomplishments vs. individual achievements. Related to the preference to work together on projects is the desire to receive recognition and appreciation *as a team*, rather than one or two team members being selected to receive individual accolades (this is similar to many Asian cultures in perspective). In fact, picking out one person as the leader of the effort can actually be offensive—both to the team and to the one receiving the attention.

Generations and work ethic

The second recurrent theme related to appreciation and generational differences is the question: ***Do younger employees really have*** *less of a work ethic?* (Being honest, the question is usually phrased more like: "What's with these younger employees . . . don't they know how to work?")

A common complaint about younger employees from their employers and supervisors is that millennials don't seem very motivated and they often don't display a good work ethic. This complaint does not just come from boomers but also is frequently voiced by managers and supervisors who are in their later thirties and forties (Gen X).

As I've worked with companies across the country with a range of age groups among their employees, three key questions have risen to the top that need to be addressed:

• **Who defines a "good work ethic"?** Supervisors and colleagues need to be aware that their view as to what a "motivated" or a "hard-working" employee looks like may be biased from their personal worldview. For example, just because a younger employee stays up into the early morning hours, and then sleeps in, does not mean they are lazy. It may mean that their schedule for working is different than yours.

Believe it or not, employers or supervisors are *not* the ultimate source of understanding what comprises a good work ethic.

BELIEVE IT OR NOT, EMPLOYERS or supervisors are *not* the ultimate source of understanding what comprises a good work ethic.

A good work ethic is defined first by one's customers. You and your employees are there to provide goods or services that your customers want or need. Therefore, what customers want defines what you try to provide, like being open when they need your assistance, providing quality service, or delivering goods when you agreed to.

Employers then develop expectations of appropriate work behaviors from their employees in order to serve their customers well. What you expect from your employees then (hopefully) reflects those behaviors that enable your company to serve your clients well. So these behaviors (showing up to work regularly, arriving on time, listening to and following directions) have nothing to do with generational bias. They are foundational to a company serving their clients well.

• **What, really, makes for a good work ethic?** Older generations (boomers and seniors) are notorious for focusing on and lecturing younger individuals about the need to have a "good work ethic." But what does that really mean? Here are the behaviors I have gathered from employers and supervisors:

1. *Showing up (regularly)*
2. *Arriving on time, ready to work*
3. *Listening to and following instructions*
4. *Willingness to learn (learning attitude)*
5. *Performing quality work (vs. "going through the motions")*
6. *Displaying a positive, "can do" attitude*
7. *Completing work in a timely fashion*
8. *Being a "hard worker."* This also needs to be specified because many assume others know what they mean when using the term. A hard worker is one who:

   a. stays on task; doesn't need close supervision to do so.
   b. puts forth consistent, good effort; not taking excessive breaks.
   c. continues to work hard even when they are tired or not supervised.
   d. completes the job given, then looks for other work to be done.

• **So, does a good work ethic look different for different generations?** As we look at this list of behaviors, the conclusion seems to be both "No" and "Sometimes." No, because the behaviors that together comprise a "good work ethic" are consistently desired by customers regardless of their generation. Sometimes, because a caveat exists: *The specific behaviors may differ according to the need (and generation) of the* *client.* For a millennial client, getting answers via a text message, an email, or through a chat room may actually be the preferred means of communication. And often they want an immediate response (maybe while they are working between 9 p.m. and 1 a.m.). In contrast, a Gen-Xer may want to schedule a call or videoconference in the next day or so, while a boomer may want to meet in person.

• **What is the problem? Why don't younger employees seem to know how to work?** I don't think it is a motivation (or caring) issue in most cases. And I think it is dangerous to judge others' thoughts and feelings.

I believe the problem stems from this question: *How do you learn how to work?*

We learn to work by *working* (and receiving instruction and feedback). It's not by watching TV or movies, and I haven't seen a video game that teaches young people how to work. (I'd love to be the creator of one, if it is possible!) Many, not all, millennials have far fewer work experiences than their cohorts from prior generations.

Generally, I believe, it is not their fault. It is ours (their parents). Why? Because many twentysomethings didn't work in high school during summers or vacation breaks (or have a part-time job). And a lot of younger adults didn't work much during college—summers or otherwise. In fact (a minority to be sure), their first "real" job (that is, not working for a relative or a friend's parent) isn't until they complete college.

The result? The development of work-related behaviors is more like that of teenagers in past generations. In essence, many (not all) twentysomething employees have far less experience working full-time than twentysomething employees did a decade or two ago. As a result, many of the lessons learned by previous generations during their teen years are being learned in the early twenties currently.

What lessons might this include?

- You are expected to show up for work every day, on time, and if you aren't coming you should call to let your supervisor know.
- You are supposed to listen to and follow the instructions given on how to do tasks, even if you think you already know what to do or you believe you have a better way to do the task.
- Generally, your input will be asked for when it is desired.
- The goal of work is to complete tasks (well), not just put in your time.
- If you complete a task early, look for something else that needs to be done or ask what you can do to help.

WHAT TO DO?

Grumbling "These young people just don't know how to work" doesn't help, so quit! Instead, employers, managers and supervisors can do the following:

First, *adjust your expectations.* Many younger workers need help learning what it means to "work hard." Don't expect them to already have a well-developed work ethic.

Secondly, *retool your training for younger employees.* Intentionally instruct them in the behaviors you desire and *explain why* they are important to the success of the organization.

Finally, *actively encourage high school and college students you know to start working earlier—and provide opportunities for them to do so.*

You have a tremendous opportunity to positively impact the next generations of workers—take it!

WHAT ABOUT GENDER?

Sometimes the big issue in exploring differences is that there *aren't* really any major differences across groups. In understanding appreciation and gender, this is the case.

When we look at the occurrence rates of the languages of appreciation on the Motivating by Appreciation Inventory, we can see how each language is chosen as a person's primary language of appreciation, secondary language of appreciation, the primary and secondary languages combined, and the least valued language of appreciation.

The information in the table below shows the prevalence rate for each appreciation language, both across all respondents and for each gender. This is from the responses of over 81,000 individuals who have taken the Motivating by Appreciation Inventory, with 66.3 percent of them being women and 33.7 percent being men.

Distribution of Languages of Appreciation from the MBA Inventory			
	ALL	FEMALE	MALE
Primary Language of Appreciation			
Words of Affirmation	47.5%	48.4%	45.8%
Quality Time	24.4%	25.3%	22.7%
Acts of Service	22.6%	20.9%	25.8%
Tangible Gifts	5.5%	5.4%	5.7%
Least Valued Language of Appreciation			
Words of Affirmation	5.2%	5.1%	5.6%
Quality Time	7.2%	7.1%	7.2%
Acts of Service	19.1%	20.7%	15.9%
Tangible Gifts	68.5%	67.1%	71.3%

As can be seen from the information reported, there is virtually no difference across men and women in the frequency they choose each language of appreciation. To be honest, this is a rather surprising finding. I would have expected *some difference somewhere.*

But the data are clear: *there are no significant differences in how often men and women prefer the different languages of appreciation.* The prevalence of how often men and women choose Words of Affirmation, Quality Time, Acts of Service, and Tangible Gifts is essentially the same.

VALUES, BACKGROUND, AND LIFE EXPERIENCES

Probably the greatest differences among employees in the workplace originate from each individual's personal background, family upbringing, cultural context, and life experiences. Even individuals who seem to be quite similar in terms of background and life experience can quickly find out they have quite dissimilar values and ways of looking at life situations.

These personal differences bring a richness to life, along with unexpected findings that can lead to tensions, even on things like whether the office should have a Christmas holiday celebration and what that should look like. Part of the maturation process in life is to learn (experientially) that not everyone thinks the same way you do or solves problems in the same manner that has worked for you, and to accept that your way of getting a task completed may not always be the only (or best?) way to do so!

LEADING THOSE WHO ARE DIFFERENT FROM YOU

Many developing leaders start out with the goal of making an army of workers and junior leaders who are like the clone armies from the Star Wars movies—where every soldier looked and acted the same

147

as the leader they were created to emulate. Sounds cool, and boosts your ego, but trying to make people to be like you is not a very effective strategy for developing a healthy team of employees who can accomplish significant goals.

Why? Because no one is all knowing and has all the skills, education and experience necessary to individually complete all aspects of the business, and even if you did, you would eventually hit the limits of your time and energy as the business grew. When you have a group of "mini-yous," you will limit what your business can accomplish. What any successful business needs are employees who bring their unique abilities, strengths, and perspectives to the challenges they will face. But to be able to draw and keep talented individuals who are different from you, you have to learn a key skill: You have to learn how to lead people who are different from you.

There are lots of great books on leadership that provide valuable insights into key skills and abilities that are needed to effectively lead others. But one concept that is not stressed enough is: *to lead a successful team, you have to understand those who are not like you, and be able to support, encourage, and motivate them.*

To truly begin to practice this leadership skill, some foundational principles need to be understood and accepted:

1. *You need others in order to accomplish the goals you are pursuing* (if not, the goals probably are not large enough). You really do need others to help accomplish the BHAG (Big Hairy Audacious Goals) you have for the company. So it would be wise to start treating others like you need them, versus reminding them how much they need you.

2. *Other people think, believe, process information, and are motivated differently than you.* Some think big picture; others need specific details. Some are analytical, while others are dreamy creative types. Some need to *see* the information; others need to *hear* it (and some need both). Some want accolades and praise; others just want a private "thanks."

3. *Doing things your way isn't always the best way.* You are bright, talented, and you get things done. But, believe it or not, your way of doing things isn't the best way for everyone else (although your way probably is the best way for you). Additionally, your way may not be the best way for some tasks to get done (for example, many engineers' ideas for marketing products aren't that effective).

4. *You need people who are different than you to make a good team.* Differences are good (although they involved challenges—like communicating clearly). You need detailed, analytic conservative fiscal types. You need energetic, outgoing "let's tackle the world" salespeople. You need people who communicate ideas effectively to others—both orally and in writing. You need people who can communicate through pictures, images, colors, and movement. You need dreamers and you need "get it done" implementers. A successful business utilizes the strengths of their multitalented team members. (Go to the FAQ section at the end of the book to read about the relationships between DISC personality styles and the appreciation languages.)

5. *Not everyone feels appreciated in the same ways.* Many leaders attempt to reward and motivate their employees in the ways that are important to *them*. If you try to use the one-size-fits-all approach, the results will be discouraging. First, you won't hit the mark if you give verbal praise to those who believe words are cheap. Secondly, you will waste a lot of time, energy and potential money giving gifts, rewards, and bonuses to those for whom a little time or camaraderie is worth more than the expensive dinner you treated them to. And finally, you will probably become irritated that your team members don't seem to "appreciate all I do for them."

Do this instead. Find out how they are motivated; what is important to them; what makes them feel valued and appreciated. And then (almost by an act of faith sometimes) do what they tell you is important to them, even if it doesn't make any sense to you. You will be pleasantly surprised at the positive results you will see.

Remember, we are all different. And how we are each unique brings strength to our workplace just like a thriving forest needs all types of shrubs, groundcover, and trees to survive the wide range of environmental challenges that will be experienced over time. Celebrate the differences you encounter—they are good for you and your organization!

REFLECTION QUESTIONS

What types of people who are different from you do you find most challenging to relate to?

When thinking about the ability to see situations from others' point of view (perspective taking), what observations do you have about the level of perspective taking others in your daily life seem to have?

How would you rate yourself in the following areas?

	Low	Medium	High
Cognitive empathy	☐	☐	☐
Emotional empathy	☐	☐	☐
Compassionate empathy	☐	☐	☐

How difficult do you find it to be to truly understand others who feel appreciated in ways other than you do?

Which of the following languages of appreciation is the most difficult for you to accept that others might want to be appreciated in that way?

Words of Affirmation	☐
Quality Time	☐
Acts of Service	☐
Tangible Gifts	☐
Physical Touch	☐

What personal experiences do you think have significantly impacted the way you view life that may lead you to have a different perspective than others you work with?

What generational differences have you observed with regard to what seems to make different generations feel appreciated?

What are your thoughts about the often-cited statement that younger employees seem to have a less well-developed work ethic?

Does it surprise you that men and women don't really differ in how frequently they chose the different languages of appreciation as their preferred language? Why or why not?

8

CAN APPRECIATION CROSS CULTURES?

Abby, the lead HR trainer for the firm, was talking with a couple of department supervisors. "I'm really pleased with how the Appreciation at Work training is going with our teams," she said. "They seem to enjoy the process; they get the concepts and are willing to try them out with their teams."

"Me too," Rob agreed, "but I've been thinking about some of the cultural differences we face between our long-term older male employees and some of the younger Hispanic team members. Each group comes from pretty different backgrounds and the older guys don't understand hardly any Spanish (let alone speak it).

"I'm just not sure how they are going to show appreciation in ways that are meaningful (or acceptable!) to someone from a different generation *and* from a culture these guys are not that familiar with."

"Yes, I know what you mean," Abby replied. "The other day, some of the guys in the shipping department were ribbing James about being a Rangers fan (he grew up in New York and he's 'hard core'), and Javier and some of the others had no idea what they were talking about because they don't follow hockey at all."

"And the guys can get pretty cutting, which can seem mean, if you aren't used to that type of teasing," Kiana added.

Rob said, "Really, the issue isn't limited to people from different countries or who speak another language. There are some real
differences between people like me, who grew up in the Northeast,
and those who are from the South. The supervisors we inherited from
Atlanta and Charleston when we merged with the other firm clearly
have a different style of relating than us 'cold New Englanders.'"
 Kiana interjected, "Well, that doesn't even begin to touch on the
differences between all the different subcultures we have here—
those from the inner city, the suburbanites, and all the different ethnic
and religious backgrounds people come from. It's pretty complicated.
I hope we can figure it out."

I have had the privilege of traveling internationally to numerous
countries to introduce the concept of authentic appreciation in the
workplace. As a result, I am often asked: "Isn't appreciation and recognition just an American issue? Are the concepts really transferrable
across different cultures?"

Fortunately, authentic appreciation and vibrant workplaces aren't
limited to certain cultures. They exist on every inhabited continent.
And different cultures bring out unique aspects of what "vibrancy"
looks like.

Interestingly, Dr. Gary Chapman's book *The 5 Love Languages*®
(from which the 5 languages of appreciation were developed) has been
incredibly embraced by dozens of cultures in every corner of the world.
The book has been translated into over fifty languages and has been enthusiastically accepted and utilized in Asian, African, Middle Eastern,
Russian, European, Latin American, and Anglo cultures. So it appears
the 5 languages conceptually "fit" across most cultures.

We have individuals from six continents who utilize our Appreciation at Work resources, and *The 5 Languages of Appreciation in the
Workplace* has been published in at least eighteen languages. As you
will see in the table on the next page, the translations represent Asia,

northern Europe, southern Europe, eastern Europe, Africa, and Latin America. (Go to the international page of the www.appreciationat-work.com website for the most recent listing and links.)

Translations of *The 5 Languages of Appreciation in the Workplace*	
Afrikaans	Chinese (simplified)
Czech	English
Danish	German
French	Indonesian
Hungarian	Korean
Italian	Portuguese
Norwegian	Spanish
Russian	Turkish
Chinese (traditional)	

THE NEED IS FELT ACROSS CULTURES

So, as demonstrated by their use in multiple languages, the constructs of the 5 languages of appreciation seem to be transferrable across cultures. But, more importantly, the *need* for appreciation in the workplace is deeply felt by leaders who work in these countries.

Regin Akkemik, an organizational trainer in Turkey, was asked by one of the large multinational firms she serves to find a resource to help them create a more positive work culture utilizing effective recognition and appreciation practices. When she found our book, she was excited, stating,

"There is a huge need for authentic recognition and appreciation in our workplaces. I'm so excited to find your resources—the book, the online inventory, and the training materials. I can see crystal clearly that learning how to speak an employee's appreciation language fluently is extremely important for today's work environment."

Additionally, Sofie Halkjaer, CEO of a strategic change-management consulting firm in Copenhagen, Denmark, was elated when she discovered the Appreciation at Work resources. She invited me to Copenhagen to speak to a major change management conference where she reported:

"The issue of appreciation in the workplace is critical for helping implement changes in an organization. The two concepts fit together beautifully. When employees feel truly appreciated, then they are more open to change, and their normal resistance response declines significantly. The 5 languages are a simple, yet effective way that easily fits into the Danish workplace."

Pat McGrath, an organizational leader in Latin America, has been instrumental in getting our materials translated into Spanish. He states: "The need is huge in Mexico, Central, and South America. Employers and supervisors are seeing they no longer can just demand that employees do what they want, but are learning that showing genuine appreciation goes a long way to keeping talented team members."

As an organizational consultant in Singapore, Jasmine Liew reports that the work culture there has created a great need for appreciation because "recognition is only meant for the top and highest performing staff, and it usually will be the same group of people who are recognized. Thus, this performance-based recognition neglects the majority of employees who are diligent, well-performing staff members."

At last count, we have had individuals from twenty-eight countries who are Certified Facilitators, using our Appreciation at Work implementation kit with organizations and businesses in their communities.

**Countries with *Appreciation at Work*
Certified Facilitators**

Australia
Bahamas
Brazil
Canada
China
Czech Republic
Denmark
England
Finland
Germany
Hungary
Korea
Kuwait
Malaysia
Mexico
Myanmar (Burma)
Netherlands
Namibia
New Zealand
Nigeria
Norway
Philippines
Poland
Singapore
South Africa
Turkey

A FRAMEWORK FOR
UNDERSTANDING CULTURAL DIFFERENCES

Cross-cultural differences, and communicating effectively across cultures, has been a huge area of social science research for decades. As a result, there are numerous ways to examine the variations of behavior and styles of communication. One helpful approach, however, provides a rather straightforward, practical way of thinking about cultural differences.

In a fascinating book *The Culture Map*, Erin Meyer outlines a model that identifies a series of characteristics of cultures and where cultures vary:

- **Communication:** Low-context (simple, clear) vs. high-context (nuanced, layered)
- **Negative feedback:** Direct vs. indirect
- **Persuasion:** Principles-first (deductive) vs. application-first (inductive)
- **Leadership:** Egalitarian (among peers) vs. hierarchical (boss/ subordinate)
- **Decision-making:** Consensus vs. top-down
- **Trust:** Task-based (cognitive) vs. relationship-based (affective)
- **Disagreement:** Confrontational vs. avoids confrontation
- **Time and scheduling:** Linear vs. flexible

Mapping out your culture (for example, the US) and the culture of origin of a business associate along these continua of traits provides insights for understanding areas of potential misunderstanding in your interactions.[1] (If you are curious how the various cultures are described, just search the Internet with the terms "The Culture Map" and [nation name].)

LESSONS FROM A
MULTINATIONAL TRAINING EXPERIENCE

A few years ago, I had the privilege of training the management and supervisors of an elite international organization in how to communicate authentic appreciation to their staff. Functioning within the tourism and hospitality industries, the staff (in one location) come from over forty countries and six continents.

As I approached the training, I was interested to see and hear if the staff desired to be appreciated for their work. Additionally, I was curious to learn the various ways employees felt comfortable receiving appreciation and what the challenges might be due to differences in the variety of cultures (for example, British, Norwegian, Filipino, Colombian, South African, Indian, Irish, Egyptian, and American).

Employees from all cultures represented affirmed that, yes, they would like to be valued for the work they do and have the appreciation communicated to them by their supervisors and colleagues. A few individuals reported that appreciation in the workplace was not part of their home culture (mainly northern European cultures—Finnish, Dutch, German). Appreciation from one's supervisor was not expected by the employee, nor did managers believe they should have to communicate appreciation.

Having translated (both linguistically and culturally) our materials into different languages, I was fairly sure that there would be differences in the *type* of appreciation desired by individuals from different cultural backgrounds. Most supervisors were familiar with the concept of saying, "Thank you" or "Good job." But the idea that there were other ways of expressing appreciation (spending quality time, doing an act of service) was new to most of the international managers.

One interesting observation was that people have fairly strong opinions about what they did *not like* in how appreciation might be communicated by others. The Brits were repulsed by the repetitive kissing on the cheeks by the southern Europeans (Portuguese, Italians). Many European women did not understand the purpose or meaning of high fives and fist bumps. And the Filipinos did not understand (and sometimes were offended by) the humor used by the British, Irish, and Americans—which was often seen as a way of communicating warmth and friendship by the senders.

One of the encouraging aspects of the training was the feedback I received from the top executives down to the frontline supervisors. The most important concepts they valued included:

- Not everyone feels appreciated in the same way;
- There are alternative ways to communicate appreciation besides words (and words are not valued by everyone);
- Communicating appreciation in the way that is valued by the *recipient* is critical, as opposed to what the sender prefers;
- Perceived authenticity is key and can be a challenge in cross-cultural work relationships.

Roy Saunderson, a colleague who has done training on recognition and appreciation in Canada, the United States, Europe, and the Middle East, made an interesting comment to me when we were discussing appreciation and cultural differences. He stated,

"Wherever I've gone, regardless of how warm and expressive or cool and distant a culture is—all the employees I interacted with indicated to me that they desired more, and more authentic recognition in their workplace."

So, it appears the answer to the opening question, "Isn't the appreciation concept really just an American fad?" is an emphatic: "No, it's not!" The need for appreciation is expressed in a variety of countries and cultures.

WHAT ABOUT REGIONAL DIFFERENCES?

Most of my work has been in the United States, but in virtually every corner and region (including Hawaii and Alaska), I've enjoyed discovering some of the unique ways individuals within geographic regions and subcultures prefer to receive appreciation and encouragement. Similar to other cultural differences, we have found that no one Language of Appreciation is more highly preferred than others in different regions of the country. But the specific actions within each appreciation language may vary some—largely related to local cultural traditions and interests: what festivals and cultural events people enjoy going to, sports teams followed (college, pro, types of sports), cultural norms for communicating appreciation publicly or privately, and so forth.

Two of the bigger differences across regions become evident in: a) relational styles and their impact on communicating appreciation; and b) the appreciation language of physical touch.

Relational styles

Generally speaking, the Northeast and Upper Midwest regions are more formal and private in their interactions with others, while the South and West are more informal and open about personal matters and communication. In New England and the Northeastern corridor, people tend to have a firmer boundary between work life and their personal lives. They are cordial to their colleagues, but they typically don't expect to develop close relationships with their coworkers, especially regarding personal and family time. (These are clearly generalizations, but still largely true.)

Conversely, those from the South (including the Southeast, the Deep South, and Southwest) are more communicative and open about their thoughts and feelings—on the surface, at least. A dynamic does occur where Southerners often will have a friendly interaction style, but they keep their deeper personal opinions to themselves and share those with only family and closest friends.

To fill in the gaps, those from the Great Lakes region and Midwest tend to be "in between" the Northeast and South—friendly, but also not telling others everything they think and feel. Our friends from the West and Northwest tend to have that West Coast free spirit and openness. If you ask, they'll tell you what they think.

The communication of appreciation in the workplace, then, follows those norms. Employees in the more formal, private regions tend to have less experience with receiving appreciation, and it can feel a bit awkward to them initially. They also can feel a bit overwhelmed with interacting with colleagues (or clients or vendors) from the South, who greet them enthusiastically and warmly (and sometimes try to hug them!). Obviously, due to their different styles, the regional cultural differences create some interaction challenges in organizations that have offices and staff across the country.

Physical Touch

From the beginning of our work, the language of Physical Touch has been the most challenging and interesting aspect of communicating appreciation in the workplace. Why? Because individuals tend to have the strongest opinions (both negative and positive) regarding physical touch in the workplace. (Rather than address all of the related issues here, please see the videos and articles on our website, www.appreciationatwork.com/learn, for a more thorough discussion.)

Parallel with the overall cultural differences, Southerners are known for being quite comfortable with hugging (sometimes "side hugs"), even in the workplace. Midwesterners are typically fine with handshakes, high fives, fist bumps, and a pat on the back. Those from the West also have developed their own variation of a half-hug/slap on the back greeting (typically used by men greeting one another). And in the Northeast, they may greet you verbally with "hey" and a nod, but any touching besides a formal handshake is not in their vocabulary. Obviously, these are broad generalizations, and there are clearly individuals from every region who have a "don't touch me—anyone, anytime, anywhere" posture (many, unfortunately, for good reason). Subcultural differences need to be noted, as well. Some ethnic groups and cultures within the United States strongly value physical touch as a form of appreciation and communication of warmth in relationships—including many Hispanics and Latin Americans, and individuals from southern Europe (Italy, Greece, Spain, Portugal).

THE 5 LANGUAGES ARE CROSS-CULTURAL, BUT ACTIONS ARE CULTURE-SPECIFIC

What we have found in applying the 5 languages of appreciation in a variety of countries, cultures, and even regions of the United States, is that while the 5 languages are easily understood and applied across cultures, *the appropriate actions within each Language of Appreciation vary significantly.*

One does not have to be outside of the United States to observe the importance of getting the specific act of appreciation correct in order to hit the target and truly impact the recipient. I had a manager say to me, "Okay, so John's language is Quality Time. What does that mean practically? What do I *do* as a result of knowing that information?" We subsequently (and fairly quickly!) revised the inventory to allow individuals to identify the specific actions preferred within their primary language. For example, a quiet administrative assistant, Kaylie, told me: "My language is Quality Time, but I don't want individual time with my supervisor. I'm fairly shy and introverted, and my supervisor is pretty intense. But I do love going to lunch with my coworkers—that is the type of time important to me."

As a result, we created the process within taking the inventory that, once the respondent's primary language of appreciation is identified, we then take them to an action item list where they can pick the specific actions most meaningful to them. These actions are then included in their individualized report.

It is always a privilege to learn from our friends across the globe. I've asked trainers to share their thoughts and impressions about the relevance of the Languages of Appreciation for their culture, and also how the approach to appreciation and specific actions differ in their work settings. We have posted these online at www.appreciationatwork.com/international. Currently, there are examples from Canada, Germany, China, Korea, Singapore, Denmark, Latin America, and Turkey.

A DEEP HUMAN NEED

The evidence is clear and resounding—the 5 languages of appreciation are applicable in multiple cultures. The focus on appreciation is *not* just an American fad, but rather reflects a deep human need experienced across the globe.

The challenge is knowing how to communicate appreciation appropriately within various cultures. We are proud to be able to say that our trainers throughout the world are helping to "translate" the 5 languages of appreciation into culturally relevant actions. Similar to the wide range of beautiful flowers and plants found across the globe, we are able to assist in creating positive workplaces in Asia, Europe, Latin America, Africa, the Middle East, and North America—all of which have their own distinctive characteristics but are healthy and vibrant in their own unique ways!

REFLECTION QUESTIONS

Does it surprise you that appreciation in the workplace fits in a variety of cultures? Why or why not?

When you read the descriptions of Meyer's cultural characteristics, where on each continuum would you place the majority US culture (or the culture with which you are most familiar) on the items below?

Communication
Low context   High context
(simple, clear)   (nuanced, layered)

Negative Feedback
Direct negative   Indirect negative

Leadership
Egalitarian   Hierarchical
(facilitator)   (boss/subordinate)

Decision-making
Consensual   Top-down

Trust
Task-based   Relationship-based
(cognitive)   (affective)

Disagreeing
Confrontational   Avoid confrontation

Time
Linear time   Flexible time

Share some of your ratings that strike you as interesting with others in your group.

What observations do you have about potential differences in how appreciation is expressed (or not expressed) in different regions of the United States?

What is your personal preference about receiving a show of appreciation through appropriate physical touch?

Which of the cross-cultural examples shared in the chapter did you find most interesting?

Section 4

EMPLOYEE CHARACTERISTICS THAT CREATE PROBLEMS

The issues addressed in Section 4 include: The final source of obstacles comes from employees themselves. The truth is that some coworkers are harder to love than others. Some people have characteristics that create challenges for their supervisors and coworkers to genuinely value them. Others, due to their low performance or *how* they achieve at higher levels, make communicating authentic appreciation difficult. The issues addressed in Section 4 include:

- Chapter 9: colleagues who, for a variety of reasons, are just difficult to authentically appreciate,
- Chapter 10: the challenges performance issues (both under performers and others create in communicating appreciation.

These chapters are then followed by answers to a number of Frequently Asked Questions (FAQs) and also a variety of resources available to use in different work settings.

9

COLLEAGUES WHO ARE HARD TO APPRECIATE

Maria sat in a follow-up group discussion for the Appreciation at Work training her division had been receiving. The conversation was lively and interesting, but Maria couldn't stop thinking about one person who was not in the room: Jonathan. How was this going to work with him? In her years at the organization, she had had difficulty connecting with her coworker. Not for the first time, she thought, *I really don't like him. What do I do?*

After the discussion came to a close, Maria approached Katie, the HR trainer who was facilitating the process, and asked if they could set a time to talk together in the next few days. Two days later, Katie and Maria found a private area where they could talk. Maria opened up the conversation: "I've really enjoyed the material on the 5 languages of appreciation and have found it to be pretty easy to start applying, except . . . I have a challenging situation that I don't know how to handle."

Katie, not too surprised, responded: "What's that? There are a number of little bumps in the road that have to be worked through."

"Well, being straightforward," Maria said, "there is one person on our team that I just don't understand. He's not a bad guy necessarily. But we don't click—we are *totally* different in how we view life and approach tasks. He's super quiet and pretty much works on his own.

I like to talk and interact—bounce ideas off people and work together with others to find the best solution. But when I talk to him or ask him a question, he just looks at me and says, 'I don't know' and goes back to work.

"I could deal with that, I guess, but there's more. He's just not that good at what he does: he's slow to get things done, there are usually mistakes that have to be corrected, and the worst part is, he *never* takes responsibility for the problem. He always has an excuse, or he blames somebody else. Like 'The printer didn't print it right' or 'I got the specs late from the design lab so I had to do the best I could in the time left.' And then he walks away with a snarky attitude. He doesn't offer to help or correct things and just expects the rest of us to deal with it.

"To be honest, at this point, I *don't* really appreciate him, and in fact, I sort of resent him and the way he creates more work for the rest of us since he doesn't do his job right."

She looked at Katie. "So how am I supposed to 'appreciate' him when I don't even like him?"

It's hard to build a vibrant, thriving workplace when you don't really like (or appreciate) those you work with. Sure, the organization may be functioning pretty well, but that may not matter at an individual level if you have to work with people who really irritate you.

When employees and supervisors are sincerely trying to understand and implement the concept of authentic appreciation, they may eventually wind up asking: "*What do I do when I don't really appreciate one of my colleagues?*"

Janice, a supervisor in a small office setting, came up to me during a break in our training session. I could sense her pain when she said:

"*Dr. White, I get it. I see the need to communicate genuine appreciation to my team—and it is needed throughout our organization. But what am I supposed to do with a person who is negative and complaining all the time? They are hard to relate to positively, let alone appreciate!"*

The individuals asking this question typically accept the importance of communicating appreciation and many times have begun to work a plan with their colleagues. But eventually they experience the reality that there are some coworkers they just don't have many positive feelings for. And they are not sure what to do—"push through" and try to communicate something positive, even if they don't really *feel* positive about the person? Put on their best encouraging face and fake it? Not do anything?

Let's take an honest look at difficult-to-appreciate colleagues and develop a plan for dealing with them in an honest, practical way.

FIRST STEP: DON'T TRY TO FAKE IT

A good friend and I were discussing appreciation in the workplace, and how the concept might apply to his workplace. He was a successful leader of a large nonprofit organization, and he told me:

"Paul, I'm not sure what to do. Right now, my staff and I aren't getting along real well. There is some tension in the office—partly due to personality characteristics, partly due to differences of opinion about how we should do things, and partly due to the fact that they aren't really doing what I asked them to. I'm wondering: Should I just go ahead and implement this?"

I responded quickly, "Steve, absolutely not! I don't think this would be a good direction to go. I would guess it is fairly obvious to them that you aren't happy with them, and trying to communicate appreciation would blow whatever trust you may have out of the water. Then you would have an even worse situation. I think you need to address the issues underlying your lack of appreciation first."

As you might infer from his description, there were a number of issues that contributed to his not valuing his staff: personality conflicts, lack of shared vision, and (as I shared with him) a lack of his holding his team members accountable to complete tasks he had given them, which was largely due to his avoidance of conflict. (We later discussed this issue and how he might grow in his ability to address difficult situations directly.)

Most people believe they have a good sense of when others are not being genuine in their compliments and praise. They think they have very sensitive radar when they believe someone is just going through the motions rather than truly meaning what they say. People frequently report comments to me like:

"He doesn't mean it. He is just acting like he appreciates me."

"I don't believe Jennifer when she tries to show me appreciation for something I've done. She is setting me up to get something she wants."

WARNING: *Don't try to judge other people's motives.* We often are not sure why *we* ourselves do certain things or make various choices. Our own motives can be mixed. Accurately determining why another person says or does something is virtually impossible.

And attempting to judge another person's reasons for acting typically brings about two negative results: other people experience us as being condescending and we open ourselves up to being judged by others. (Remember the saying, "People who live in glass houses shouldn't throw stones"?) When people feel judged, they often respond defensively with "Yeah, but *you* . . ." The result? Conflict. Hurt feelings. A relational mess.

The better course of action when you question another person's motives is to give them the benefit of the doubt. If, in fact, a colleague does have an ulterior motive for their action, usually the truth becomes evident over time.

(For a more thorough discussion of a lack of genuineness, go to chapter 3, "Why Recognition Programs Don't Work.")

WHY SOME COLLEAGUES ARE HARD TO VALUE: WHAT EMPLOYEES SAY

Let's be honest, some people are more difficult to work with than others. There are irritable colleagues, those who don't follow through on tasks, and people we just don't understand. Also, certain types of people are tougher to value for some people than others. For example, I have trouble encouraging really shy, introverted colleagues, while it isn't a problem for my customer service manager to do so.

To gain a better understanding of what makes some colleagues more challenging to appreciate, we conducted a survey and asked, "What makes it difficult to appreciate a colleague?" From hundreds of replies to the survey, we found a number of themes.

The top ten characteristics described by the respondents follow, with example responses from the survey. Difficult to appreciate colleagues are:

1. *Chronically negative* (16.4% of the examples given).
 • "It's difficult to appreciate the people who are always complaining! It can be hard to find the good in them and express appreciation, especially when I know they are going to react negatively or blow it off completely."
 • "The colleagues I find the most difficult to appreciate are the angry or resistant ones. There are those who take every opportunity to complain about the workplace or who begin (or bring to a halt) conversations about new changes or ideas with dismissive attitudes and phrases like 'I'm not doing that.'"
 • It's challenging when a colleague regularly has a nasty disposition or refuses to do anything outside the realm of their job description. Their tendency toward general unpleasantness and unwillingness to step up when needed makes it very hard for others to appreciate them.

2. *Arrogant and self-absorbed* (13.6 %)

• These are the colleagues who require that they be the center of attention, the only person in the room, the one whose ideas are the best, the only voice in discussions, and who take the credit. Such individuals are often charming, witty, and smart, but eventually come across as disrespectful, tiring, and annoying.

• I have a problem with coworkers who think they know it all or are better than others. They might take over on a project, become pushy or exclusive, and are unwilling to collaborate or share.

3. *Inflexible and not collaborative* (10.0%).

• I find it difficult to appreciate colleagues when they are unwilling to work collaboratively. They feel their way is the only way and they are not flexible. When people won't compromise, the ball stops rolling and it is frustrating for everyone.

• There are those people who don't embrace the teamwork attitude or show common courtesy—a coworker choosing not to respond to an email or voicemail, or making an excuse when asked to help with something.

4. *Poor work ethic or poor performance* (8.8%).

• My least favorite are those who don't pull their weight and try to get away from their responsibilities.

• Some colleagues do not perform their expected job duties, and then, whenever possible, take credit for the work that others have done.

• I find it hard to see the good in coworkers who complain about being busy but constantly waste time.

5. *Not trustworthy; lack of follow-through* (7.8%).

• Colleagues who fail to deliver on their promises and commitments are tough to collaborate with and appreciate.

• I have a coworker who doesn't pay attention to detail. She will not admit when she makes a mistake and always makes excuses for shoddy work. It is difficult for me to show appreciation when a task is completed because often, her team members are fixing her mistakes.

• I struggle to appreciate a coworker who is inconsistent. While he might do well once in a while, his work is not consistently done well or at an acceptable level.

6. (tie) *Dismissive of appreciation given* **(6.6%).**

• When a colleague discounts appreciation and deflects praise, it is tough! When I share words of affirmation in the form of catching someone doing something right, the most challenging colleague says it was "no problem," "not a big deal," or "someone else should get the praise."

• I have an employee who is basically Eeyore, the donkey in *Winnie-the-Pooh*. He hardly says anything and when he does it is usually negative about his work or situation. Any appreciative remark given to him is cast aside.

• Colleagues can be difficult to appreciate when they are dismissive of expressions of gratitude or admiration, especially if the dismissiveness appears to come from a sense of arrogance.

7. (tie) *A lack of social connection or personality difference* **(6.6%).**

• When a person's work style is opposite from mine it is hard to step back and appreciate the differences they bring to the table to benefit the greater whole.

• I think we're naturally drawn to people we have a connection with; people with whom we can relate. When that connection doesn't exist, it's difficult to appreciate them on a personal level.

8. *Disrespectful, condescending attitude toward others* **(5.4%).**

• I find colleagues who are condescending, fake, or insincere difficult to appreciate. No one wants to work with someone who makes them feel like they are insignificant, unimportant, uneducated, or irrelevant.

• In my experience, when people are condescending, I find that I avoid any kind of interaction with them or any initiative to work together on a team project. It's almost as though their goal is to accentuate their abilities while eroding others' self-esteem.

9. *Not being reciprocal in helping or showing appreciation* (5.0%).

• I dislike showing appreciation to a person who has no appreciation for me. I enjoy engaging with individuals who contribute to the common good, who behave like part of the team, and treat everyone with respect and appreciation.

• I've come across some colleagues who are not genuine when they attempt to encourage me. It's obvious they would rather not interact.

10. *Being extremely private* (4.0%).

• If a team member tends to be very private and does not openly share things about themselves, it's much harder to be sure you're providing appropriate appreciation. It is awkward to ask her how she would like to be appreciated, but I feel if I don't ask, I risk acting in a way that is ineffective or even damaging. Or, I could do nothing at all, which is really sad.

• Most often I struggle with not knowing what my colleagues truly do appreciate. Some do not trust me when I do try to show appreciation. It's tough to know who likes "public" and who needs "private" appreciation, and how often to show it.

The problem of the easily offended coworker

In addition to these ten characteristics that were identified from our survey, I also have found that colleagues who seem easily offended are also challenging to work with, and their sensitivity seems to be related to their language of appreciation.

In the process of training thousands of employees in the concepts of authentic appreciation, we have found that **a person's primary lan-**

guage of appreciation is often the language in which they are most easily offended!

So if you have a colleague or supervisor who seems to get upset easily and for little reason, you may want to check out what their primary language of appreciation is. It may give you some clues on some underlying relational dynamics. Let's look at each language and see what may be going on:

• *Words of Affirmation.* People who value words of praise are also easily *negatively* impacted by verbal comments. Essentially, words are their primary communication channel, and the messages are received as more intense than by those for whom words aren't as important. The implication? Even appropriate corrective instructions can feel hurtful to these individuals—and clearly casual sarcastic comments wound them. What should you do? Be more gentle with corrective feedback with these people; it doesn't take as much "oomph" to get their attention. Be sure you are also giving plenty of specific praise, as well.

©Glasbergen
glasbergen.com

"I've seen the error of my ways and I've decided to start being more respectful to my coworkers. Hey, bozo, I'm talking to you!"

• *Quality Time.* Remember, "time" doesn't always mean that the employee wants time with their supervisor. Some do. Some don't; they prefer to go out to lunch or after work with their colleagues. Those who feel valued when others spend time with them can be offended in three primary ways:

a) A supervisor schedules a meeting with the employee and repeatedly reschedules, cancels, or totally forgets the meeting. This clearly communicates that other things are more important to the manager than the individual in question.

b) A coworker or group of coworkers leaves the person out (either intentionally or unintentionally—the result is the same) when they go out to lunch or invite a group of people for a social event. Quiet colleagues can be just as offended by perceived rejection as more outgoing folks. Even introverts like to be invited and participate in social gatherings with a small group of friends.

c) Someone doesn't give them full attention when they're meeting one-on-one. Looking at text messages, checking emails, answering the phone, letting someone interrupt—all say to the person, "You're not that important."

• *Acts of Service.* Individuals who value acts of service live by the motto "actions speak louder than words." *Showing* them that they are important by doing something to help them out (especially if they are in a time crunch) is far more important than anything you could say. So how are these employees offended? One way is to just give them compliments, but never do anything *to at least offer* to help them. The other offensive action is to give them input on how they could do the task differently (or "better"), *especially* if you are just standing there watching them do the task!

• *Tangible Gifts.* People who are encouraged when they receive something tangible are primarily impacted by the facts that: a) you thought about them; b) you took time and effort to get them something; and c) you (hopefully) have gotten to know what they like. Interestingly, people who value gifts aren't necessarily upset if they don't receive something (although they may be if they never get *anything* over a long period of time). What *does* offend them is when everyone gets the same item: it is the personal nature of the gift that is meaningful to them. This appears to be why so many employees really aren't that enthralled with the "pick your gift from the catalog" approach to recognition—it's impersonal (and it didn't cost the giver anything!).

• *Physical Touch.* As you may remember, physical touch is rarely an employee's primary language of appreciation in the majority North American culture. But that is not necessarily true for all employees, and clearly not the case in other cultures (Latin American, some European). In the United States and Canada, it is probably easier to offend someone by touching a colleague (who doesn't want to be touched at all, touched by *you*, or touched in that manner or setting). But for those for whom touch is important, you can create a negative reaction by acting cool and defensive, treating them like they are "weird," and especially if you attribute negative intentions to their gesture of warmth. This is obviously a sensitive issue, so "if in doubt, don't."

Hopefully, this gives you some clues on understanding why some of your coworkers may be reacting coolly toward you—and gives you some action steps to try to improve your relationship with them!

UNIQUE CHALLENGE: TOXIC ACHIEVERS

When we were exploring what makes a workplace toxic and how workers in those settings can survive working in one, my colleagues and I came upon an interesting phenomenon—individuals who are highly skilled in their professional expertise, and who often are the highest achievers within their organization but who, at the same time, are poisonous to their work environment and damaging to those who work with them. We have come to identify these individuals as *toxic achievers.*[1]

Toxic achievers pose a serious dilemma for business owners, managers, and supervisors. On the one hand, they get the job done—quickly, and more successfully, than their peers. Their work production or sales numbers look great. But, on the other hand, they create major headaches due to the way they relate to others, their negative attitude, and their propensity to frequently want exceptions to company policies and procedures.

How do you know if one of your team members is a toxic achiever, or just a pretty good producer who can be irritating to work with? Let me describe some common characteristics.

Toxic achievers . . .

• *Are brighter, faster, and more productive than anyone else in their area within the organization.* From a production point of view, they are "top dog." They know it. You know it. The management knows it. And they use this position to their advantage.

• *Relate to others in a condescending, brusque manner, flaunting their productivity as a reason to be treated as special.* Toxic achievers are good at what they do, and they are not shy about reminding others of their performance history. They freely share their advice with colleagues (even when it is not asked for), and they refer to input from others as "stupid" (and tell them so publicly).

• *Can be angry, vindictive, and destructive with their words.* These individuals can chew you up and spit you out in one motion, either in private (if you're lucky) or in front of your peers and supervisor. They speak their mind bluntly, and their comments are amazingly cutting and derogatory.

• *Have no compunction about using others to help them accomplish their goals.* In their mind, since they are so successful, it makes sense for others in the organization to serve them so that they can become even more successful ("for the good of the organization," of course)!

• *Believe they are above the rules.* Rules, policies, and procedures are for "normal" workers, not high achievers like them. Standard procedures and paperwork just get in the way of them being able to achieve more, so they should be able to go around procedures or have someone else take care of everything for them. (This includes paperwork, expense reports, how vacation time is calculated, or going through the correct channels to request resources.)

• *Create frequent turnover in staff around them.* Whether it is their administrative assistant, clerical support for the team, their colleagues, their supervisor, or others in departments that have to collaborate with them, a revolving door of staff develops around the toxic achiever. *Nobody* wants to work with or for them for long.

• *Incite conflict among their supervisor and managers—about how best to deal with them.* Eventually, heated discussions occur between the toxic achiever's supervisor and other department heads or high-level managers. Often the managers want to keep them because their production numbers are so high (and *they* don't have to work with them on a day-to-day basis).

What can you do with toxic achievers?

What do you do with an employee who is a top performer in their field but is toxic to everyone around them? Do you keep them? Do you try to work around them?

The question eventually becomes: *Can we be successful with this person as part of our organization and/or can we realistically survive without them?* Some managers see them as irreplaceable because of their expertise, skill set, and output. Others see the collateral damage the toxic achiever creates through increasing internal tension and conflict within the company, "pushing the limits" regarding not following rules and policies, and the cost of continually having to hire new staff around them.

Ultimately, you must get rid of the toxic achiever if you're going to have a healthy organization. Until they are gone, chaos and conflict will continue (they will create it) and they aren't going to change without a dramatic life-changing experience (so don't hold your breath for that).

Toxic achievers are like a large black walnut tree that produces pounds and pounds of walnuts but nothing else can grow near the tree due to the toxicity of its leaves and root system. *They* produce, but nothing else lives.

One of the main reasons toxic achievers have to go is because the work environment will not heal and become healthy until they are gone (kind of like having to get a splinter out of your finger). No other course of action works. They are who they are and they bring the associated positive and negative results with them.

ULTIMATELY, YOU MUST get rid of the toxic achiever if you're going to have a healthy organization.

Rarely is the survival of the organization dependent on them (unless they have core knowledge or key relationships necessary for the existence of the company). It's wise not to let them get to that point of power.

It is important to note that expelling the toxic achiever from the system requires documenting their negative impact on non-"productive" areas, such as their unwillingness to follow rules and procedures, or their inability to work collaboratively with others. Otherwise, you are setting yourself up for a lawsuit once they are dismissed.

Once the toxic achiever is gone, you and those who worked with them will begin to realize how poisoned you felt and how much better life at work is with them gone. In fact, one can argue that getting rid of a toxic achiever communicates appreciation to the other employees— that you value them enough to make a tough decision so they can have a healthy workplace.

APPRECIATION COMES FROM VALUING

Learning about the different types of colleagues who are difficult to appreciate is fine, but we are still left with the issue: *What do I do when I don't appreciate someone?*

As we stated earlier, ***don't try to fake it.*** That course of action typically doesn't go well, and perceived inauthenticity will undermine any trust that may exist in the relationship.

Related to this, *don't try to push through it and make yourself appreciate a colleague.* What we have learned over time is that to appreciate someone is both a heart issue and a behavior. And, like any feeling we may experience, you can't force yourself to appreciate someone. However, similar to our other feeling responses, there are ways to make it *more likely* that we will eventually have heartfelt appreciation.

The key is valuing that person in some way. The source of appreciation is when we value something about another person: who they are, what they are able to do, what they know, character qualities. When you don't or can't appreciate someone, look and see what about them you might value.

You might value the fact that they know how to search for information well on the Internet. Or that they have experience and knowledge about your industry and competitors. It could be anything that makes them a better employee than if they didn't have that knowledge, skill, or experience.

But, especially with difficult-to-appreciate employees, *the characteristic may not be related to work.* You may find it helpful that Sarah is really good at finding deals through Craigslist, or using Groupon coupons. From getting to know one of your coworkers, you may be amazed at the vast amount of knowledge he knows about British rock groups in the '90s, or about growing vegetables organically, or whatever the topic may be.

Similarly, you may be impressed with how committed your administrative assistant is to her children and what an amazing mother she is. Or that your IT guy trains for triathlons. You may enjoy and value the cheerful demeanor one of your team members has, and how their laugh brings a smile to your face.

The point is: when you are having a hard time finding something to appreciate about another team member, look for something positive in their life, whether it is related to work or not, and bring attention to that characteristic or behavior.

FINAL THOUGHTS ON DEALING WITH DIFFICULT COLLEAGUES

Let me share a few final thoughts on what to do with someone who's hard to work with:

Do some self-reflection. Think about some potential reasons why you have a hard time appreciating this colleague. What about them don't you like? What do they do that irritates you? What about them don't you understand? Are the issues SO big that you can't think of anything they do that you appreciate? Don't let some negative characteristics blind you to their strengths.

Get to know them a little bit better. Valuing someone is difficult when you don't really know much about them. Often, finding out some about their personal history enables you to understand them more. And getting to know a bit more about their hobbies and life outside of work can lead to some areas of connection.

And remember: *you* may be difficult to appreciate for some of your colleagues!

Finally, you may experience an unexpected benefit by trying to find ways to communicate appreciation to difficult colleagues—you may (it is not guaranteed) actually begin to truly feel appreciation for them! Research (and many people's personal experience) has demonstrated that feelings about a person or situation can actually change *as a result of* behaving and thinking differently.

Don't ever forget that *you*—your actions, reactions, and attitudes—have a major influence on the level of vitality and health of your work environment!

REFLECTION QUESTIONS

When, if ever, are you tempted to try to *act like* you appreciate someone when you may be struggling to *genuinely* value them?

What experiences have you had in working with others who have been difficult?

When do you have challenges questioning the motives of others?

Which of the following coworker characteristics are difficult for you to feel positively about?

- [ ] Chronically negative
- [ ] Arrogant and self-absorbed
- [ ] Inflexible and not collaborative
- [ ] Poor work ethic or poor performance
- [ ] Not trustworthy, lack of follow-through
- [ ] Dismissive of appreciation given
- [ ] A lack of social connection or personality difference
- [ ] Disrespectful, condescending attitude toward others
- [ ] Not being reciprocal in helping or showing appreciation
- [ ] Being extremely private

When someone tries to show appreciation and you don't believe they are genuine, how do you feel?

What do you think about the idea that appreciation flows from valuing another person? How might this apply to your relationship with others at your workplace?

Does the concept of a person's preferred appreciation language being the way they are most easily offended, make sense to you? Have you ever experienced this yourself? If you are willing, please share an example.

Have you had experience with someone you believed was a toxic achiever? What was "toxic" in how this coworker behaved? What lessons did you learn from the experience?

Is there currently someone in your workplace whom you find it difficult to appreciate? What about them do you find it difficult to value?

What steps cited at the end of the chapter do you think would help you in starting to value this colleague?

- [ ] Do some self-reflection on what about them is difficult to value, and think about other positive characteristics they have.
- [ ] Consider characteristics not directly related to work performance.
- [ ] Get to know them better.

10

PERFORMANCE ISSUES: UNDERACHIEVERS, OVERACHIEVERS, AND EVERYTHING IN BETWEEN

"Rick, you've got to help me out," Stevo complained as he burst into Rick's office.

"What?" Rick glanced up from the budget he was working on, somewhat exasperated by the interruption.

"C'mon, man. How am I supposed to use this appreciation stuff with my team when you know I have a couple of real challenges to work with? You know that I've been tracking Damien for weeks now and how he is not carrying his weight. I've been documenting the mistakes he makes, how he repeatedly comes late to work, and the fact that he doesn't even come close to meeting his performance goals. And now I'm supposed to tell him I appreciate him? You've got to be kidding me!"

"Calm down." Rick motioned Steve to sit down. "I know that he has been a challenge, and I'm sorry that he landed on your team."

"Yeah, thanks a lot."

"And I know it's weird to think about trying to appreciate somebody who is creating a bunch of headaches for you, that you have to follow around and clean up their messes," Rick said. "But just cool down and we'll talk to Jen in HR and see what suggestions she has."

"Well . . . Damien isn't my only problem." Rick looked quizzical.

Steve continued, "You know Rachel, right?"

"Sure, she's the top performer on your team—and even across the whole department. How's that a problem?" Rick inquired.

Steve sighed. "Yeah, she closes more sales than anyone else and she brings in the money for the company. But she is a *pain* to work with—a *royal* pain. In fact, no one wants to work with her. The account managers complain that she bosses them around and makes them do some of the paperwork that *she* is supposed to do. But she says she doesn't have time, and that the paperwork gets in the way of her making more sales calls.

"Now," he went on, "she is telling me that she has worked so many evenings and weekends going to conferences that she deserves an extra week off over the holidays."

"Just tell her that's not company policy," Rick replied matter-of-factly.

"Easy for you to say. She's not asking me for the time off," Steve explained. "She is essentially threatening that if she doesn't get it, she'll quit and go work for one of our competitors—and take her customer relationships with her. I just can't risk that. Then *my* job would be on the line.

"Oh . . . and in the meantime, I'm supposed to tell her I appreciate her?" Steve shot Rick a look. "Like that is going to happen."

A vibrant workplace has a number of important core characteristics, but one is readily apparent: work gets done. Sometimes leaders (especially managers and executives) assume that, because I talk a lot about appreciating others in the workplace, I am all about relationships (being a psychologist probably doesn't help!). Along with this, they incorrectly conclude that I am not focused on the "business side" of work and just want everyone to be happy.

Nothing could be further from the truth. In fact, I react strongly to those in the field who focus solely on "being positive" without a corresponding understanding that work is about . . . well, work. Businesses and organizations exist to serve their customers and clientele, and they need financial resources to continue to do so. And I come unglued when I hear about Chief Happiness Officers—which I predict will fade into the sunset fairly quickly. No one is responsible for anyone else's happiness, and focusing on trying to make others happy will fail.

So let's clear the air here and now. Work is about work—getting tasks done and serving your customers. Work is not *primarily* about relationships, except as relationships help achieve the goals of the organization (or unless the task of your work is relationship building). The reality is, however, that healthy relationships *are* a key to successful organizations—relationships with clients, vendors, and those within the organization. For a work environment to be healthy, vibrant, and growing, attention has to be given to both the tasks of work and the relationships at work—because people work together to achieve the organization's goals.

THE INTERRELATIONSHIP BETWEEN PERFORMANCE, RECOGNITION, AND APPRECIATION

The challenge of dealing with employee performance issues cannot be unraveled without understanding how employee recognition, performance, and appreciation are intertwined. Like a car engine that has both gas-powered systems and electronically driven components, the two systems are interrelated. Both the gasoline driven engine and the electrical system have to work well independently but they also must coordinate their efforts together for the car to fully function properly.

Performance is important, but . . .

Let's first look at the importance of and challenges associated with focusing on the performance level of your team members. One defini-

189

tion of work is "providing goods and services that others want and are willing to pay for." You have to get the tasks done in the time frame desired by the client, at an acceptable quality level, for a price they are willing to pay, while managing the organization to be able to sustain itself financially.

But a basic challenge in working together with others is that not everyone performs at the same level with regard to the quality and amount of work done. Within a team, you will probably have at least one high achiever, a few above average employees, a group of solid team members in the middle, and then some who are not performing up to the level expected.

High and above average. Team members who are "stars," exceed their goals, and are largely self-motivated are great to have on your team. As a supervisor, you instruct them, give them the resources they need, point them in the right direction, and let them go. But, in actuality, there are a couple of challenges in communicating appreciation to your above average employees.

First, as a supervisor, it is easy to neglect them (especially the high-end achievers). They are sailing along and doing fine, so you let them be. Pretty soon, they can feel taken for granted and that you *expect* them to perform at a high level, all the time. Wise leaders continue to support, encourage, and show their high achievers how valued they are.

Separating recognition and rewards for performance from appreciation for them as a person is the second challenge. This is difficult on both ends—for the sender *and* the receiver. It can take effort for a supervisor to think about and call attention to those positive characteristics not related to achievement. And many high achievers have a hard time separating their self-worth from performing well, so the message has to be clear: "This isn't about meeting your goals. I appreciate *you as a person.*"

But even more important are the next group of employees: those who are critical to a successful organization but often get overlooked. They are the . . .

Average achievers. The group of employees that supervisors *should* be concerned about is the larger group of "middle" employees. They aren't high-performing stars. But they aren't the lowest performers. They are your average Adam and Annie who are solid and help get the work done.

The middle employees are those 50–60 percent who generally do their work but aren't going to be recognized as top performers. I liken them to the linemen and linebackers on a football team. They aren't the star quarterbacks and running backs who score most of the points, but they are critical to having a solid team. Another analogy would be that the middle group of employees is like the flour and eggs in a baking recipe. If all you have are spices and icing, you don't have much of a cake!

These are the employees who need appreciation for their "day-in, day-out" work on mundane, non-flashy tasks. If you lose your middle employees, you will struggle to perform well as a team. Often, when encouraged and treated with respect, a number of the middle workers move up and become key team players important to the success of the organization.

Conversely, if neglected and ignored they will either sink into the lower ranks of performance as a result of discouragement and not feeling valued, or they will quit and move on to another place where they hope to be appreciated for their contributions.

You don't want this to happen. So I suggest the following:

Support and encourage those reliable employees who are not performing well. Everyone needs encouragement. Stay true to your standards and don't let them slide, but remember some people may have other things going on in their lives that may be impacting their performance. Be firm but kind.

Focus on shaping their behavior in the right direction. Don't try to move them from a C+ player to an A- star. It's like teaching soccer to little kids—you can't just praise them when they score a goal (it may not happen all season!), but you praise them when they are kicking the ball to a team member. At work, if they get part of the task done correctly, mention that piece and then add one specific thing they could do slightly better.

Underachievers/low performers. A "straw-man" argument is a proposition that someone sets up as a false argument to, at least temporarily, erect an obstacle and distract from the real issues and concerns. Arguing about how or whether to show appreciation to low performers is the straw-man argument here.

Many managers who seem foundationally against appreciation in the workplace often raise the objection: "Right, so I'm supposed to appreciate an employee who doesn't do their job?" (Often, not wanting to show appreciation to *anyone* seems to be the real reason for this objection.)

In spite of this, leaders need to understand that the issue touches two sensitive areas, one related to performance, and the other to the intrinsic worth of the person. This creates a difficult point of tension. First, low performers need to be managed by holding them accountable to the standards they are supposed to meet. Eventually, either their performance will improve or they won't stay around long (whether voluntarily or involuntarily). On the other hand, the employee still has value as an individual, and coworkers may appreciate them for non-work-related characteristics, as described below.

PEOPLE ARE NOT JUST WORK UNITS

While performing one's job as expected is critical, I firmly believe that people have worth and value no matter their level of performance. Every person is a unique individual created by God, and we all are intrinsically valuable—apart from what we do or accomplish.

Many employees at all levels, including managers and supervisors, have shared with me their feelings of resentment about getting attention or hearing positive comments only when they meet or exceed the goals set for them. They feel they are viewed solely as a work unit on a spreadsheet.

This is especially true for those who are in a strong performance/reward work environment. They report feeling like their supervisors don't know them or care about them as a person. In fact, in working with one company and their call center staff, the challenge of differentiating between recognition for performance and appreciating them as individuals became a significant issue we had to discuss and work through. One supervisor shared his struggles:

It is actually hard on both ends of the spectrum—both with high achievers and low performers—to not focus solely on their performance. And we have such a strong reward system for meeting goals that, even when I try to call attention to an action or characteristic that isn't directly related to meeting their goals, I think my team members still have a hard time hearing (and maybe, believing) that it's not all about performance.

It's not that people want to be praised all the time for doing what they are supposed to do, but it is nice to hear a "thanks" or an acknowledgment when you are doing your job. Otherwise, most of the feedback employees get from supervisors comes when they make a mistake, don't meet a deadline, or aren't performing in the way desired. (Do we cease to have value when we make a mistake?)

We are more than "producers." We are people. We have personality characteristics, as well as other talents and skills that bring value to life, but may not be directly productivity-enhancing. We must not forget that employees are people (first) who have physical bodies, emotional reactions, goals and desires, as well as families and lives outside of work. When we lose this perspective, then a mechanistic, "people are just resources" workplace develops. And no one wants to work there.

UNDERSTANDING WHAT RECOGNITION
IS AND WHAT IT ACCOMPLISHES

How does improving performance relate to recognition? Businesses operate on goal setting (either explicitly or implicitly). Workers, departments, and divisions often set their own goals, as well. Research over decades has shown that recognizing and rewarding employees for reaching target goals related to their work responsibilities can be effective in improving performance.

Recognition has been defined as "to acknowledge or take notice of." Employee recognition, more specifically, calls attention to a desired action or result obtained in the workplace. An employee's performance in the area will improve when the tasks are clearly defined and understood, goals for their behaviors are set, attention is called to the employee when they demonstrate the desired behaviors, and when the employee receives an expected reward for the behavior.

Employee recognition, when designed appropriately and implemented consistently, should:

- Increase the frequency and quality of behaviors that help the organization function well and achieve its goals.
- Reward (psychologically, socially, and tangibly) the individual for their efforts.
- Motivate and incentivize others toward desired behaviors.

Really, that's it. We want employees to do what they should do, consistently, more frequently, and with appropriate quality. *The primary purpose of recognition activities is to call attention to and reward desired behaviors and results.* And when that is the purpose recognition is used for, good outcomes follow.

Unfortunately, some have tried to use recognition to achieve results it was not designed to do (and doesn't do well). For example, leaders should not try to use an employee recognition program to make individuals feel valued, create positive staff interactions, or improve peer relationships. That isn't what recognition is designed for, and thus, these results typically don't occur as a result of rewarding employees for reaching performance goals.

©Glasbergen
glasbergen.com

**"I always give 110% to my job.
40% on Monday, 30% on Tuesday, 20% on
Wednesday, 15% on Thursday, and 5% on Friday."**

An important point to note is that most employee recognition programs use some tangible gift (usually cash) as the primary, if not sole, reward for reaching performance goals. While an employee is highly unlikely to refuse the cash award, research actually shows that money is not the best motivator for high performance.[1,2]

In fact, after delivering a keynote address to the Recognition Professionals International annual conference, a good friend and colleague, Roy Saunderson, founder of Recognition Management Institute, mentioned to me that many in the world of human resources and recognition are still primarily locked into the belief that rewards (tangible gifts) are the primary motivator of performance, even though research clearly has shown that this is frequently not the case. Roy stated:

"Lots of people don't really think about the difference between

recognition and appreciation—they are stuck on the idea that employees want 'stuff,' and, as a result, companies waste millions of dollars giving out things people don't really want."

As stated previously, we have found that less than 10 percent of employees choose receiving a tangible gift as the primary means they want to be shown appreciation for what they do. It seems leaders easily fall into the trap of seeing people as production machines (put in the coin, out comes the work); or, worse, mice baited with cheese.

UNDERSTANDING WHAT
APPRECIATION IS AND WHAT IT IS FOR

Recognition and appreciation differ. While recognition focuses on performance, appreciation can mean "to understand the worth or importance of (something or someone); to admire and value; or to be grateful for something." Although appreciation can *include* an act of recognition, true appreciation for someone comes from a deeper source—appreciation flows when we value someone.

Therefore, the goals of recognition and appreciation differ. *The primary purpose of appreciation is to communicate and affirm the value of the individual.* Importantly, appreciation for a colleague is *not* always directly related to work performance. That is, we have found that coworkers may value something about their team member, and communicate appreciation for them even if their team member isn't a top producer.

To be honest, this blows some supervisors' and managers' minds. But let me give a couple of concrete examples. Do you appreciate working with someone who is cheerful, rather than one who is grumpy and negative? Or, do you value a team member who keeps their cool in the midst of a heated team meeting, and doesn't respond in ways that escalate the intensity of the "discussion"? Neither characteristic may be directly related to their performance level, but they are valued attributes.

Thus, the goals of authentic appreciation include communicating a sense of value for individuals, assisting team members in developing encouraging and supportive relationships, and aiding the organization in being able to reach its goals.

WHICH IS BETTER?

Some may ask: "Which is better: recognition or appreciation?" The answer is: *it depends*. Whether the focus should be recognition or appreciation depends on what your goals are, and what you are trying to accomplish. What those goals are varies widely. Among them:

- to make as much money as possible, as quickly as possible;
- to provide, as cheaply as possible, goods or services that customers want or need;
- to provide quality goods and valued services to your clientele in ways consistent with your core values;
- to live according to those core values, believing that you can gather others with similar perspectives to change how things are normally done.

Goals are not inherently good, better, or best. An individual's or organization's goals are rooted in and grow out of their values—what is important to them. Sometimes, in fact, the answer will vary for the same person depending on the circumstances. If your organization is struggling to survive financially, you had better emphasize increased production, or there won't be any employees to value.

Conversely, if the community has experienced a significant traumatic event, such as a natural disaster, being overly focused on productivity and not communicating that you are thankful your employees are safe won't bode well for inspiring loyalty.

The best results occur in an organization when the focus is

"both/and" rather than "either/or." Who wouldn't want a high level of productivity *and* for team members to also feel valued by their managers and one another?

For some business leaders, only recognition will make sense to them. If the leadership is solely focused on productivity and profitability, the leaders will probably not see how appreciation fits in, even though helping employees feel appreciated will most likely facilitate the company achieving those goals. Or, unfortunately, some do see the benefits but they try to use appreciation solely as a manipulative tool to increase productivity (which ultimately doesn't work).

The point? Depending on a leader's or organization's core values, their goals for the organization, and how they pursue those objectives, *understanding how the purposes of recognition and the goals of appreciation differ will aid leaders in making better choices of whether, how, and when to use each set of activities.*

Who wouldn't want a high level of productivity and for team members to also feel valued by their managers *and* one another?

The key is to match the right activity with its accompanying goals. Recognition activities that are well thought through, designed, and implemented can significantly increase most workers' performance.

I have worked with companies with well-designed, performance-based recognition programs that reward productive activity and consistently support and encourage top-quality service to their customers, while also generating revenue. In spite of this, these companies often have a morale problem because people only were recognized and rewarded when they met or exceeded their production goals. They didn't feel valued as people. We were able to correct this by taking teams through the Appreciation at Work training process, helping them communicate appreciation *in addition to* their successful performance recognition program.

Also, appreciation can enhance and support productivity. Communicating authentic appreciation to a colleague in the way that is meaningful to them can encourage them to stick with it, and will improve the quality of your relationship with them. I myself have experienced this. Our company was in the midst of a website revision and technology upgrade. As is sometimes the case (I'm being nice to our computer programming friends), we experienced some bumps in the road including disruption of service to our clients (the website didn't work and neither did the Contact Us page), the revision had gone over budget, and the launch was several weeks behind schedule. At one point I wasn't sure how much damage to our business we were going to experience. I was tired and discouraged. One of my team members saw my discouragement and communicated some very specific encouraging words to me and about the situation. (My primary language of appreciation? Words of Affirmation—and he knew this.) Immediately I felt better, and was ready to keep plugging away at the problem. And my loyalty to him as a friend grew.

MISMATCHES

Trying to use appreciation or recognition for the wrong purpose will not work, and very likely may have negative results. In many cases, this is what has been happening in the world of employee recognition.

Employee recognition activities are designed to reward desired behaviors or attain performance goals. They were not originally intended to help individuals feel valued at a personal level. Unfortunately, recognition is often inaccurately described to an organization's leadership as something that will promote a sense of appreciation, improve employee relationships, and create a positive work environment. The problem is, performance-oriented recognition *doesn't* deliver on these personal and relational goals. That is why so many employees become jaundiced toward company-wide recognition programs.

I've had friends and participants in our Appreciation at Work training report:

"Even though I got an award, I resent the process because the person giving me the award said they appreciate me. They don't even know me! They couldn't pick me out in a crowd. And they have no idea what I really do. It was bogus."

The converse can also be true. When appreciation is communicated to affirm the value of an individual with no regard to their work-related behavior, weirdness sets in. Appreciating some character quality a person displays even when it isn't work-related can be appropriate. For example, we can rejoice with a colleague and affirm them for placing well in last weekend's half marathon. This is usually a good thing. But if the celebration and discussion continue for a half hour while the person is also behind in their work, this doesn't make sense. Resentment will grow among other team members who are working hard to get their tasks done while all *you* are talking about is Jane's running performance.

RECOGNITION AND APPRECIATION: UNDERSTANDING THEIR PURPOSES

We began in this chapter discussing performance-related issues. Dealing with employees who function at a variety of levels in their jobs can make communicating appreciation challenging. This becomes even more complicated within a work setting that has a strong performance-based recognition program.

Remember that a foundational difference between employee recognition and authentic appreciation is the fact that they each have different purposes. The primary goal of recognition is *to call attention to and reward desired behaviors and results.* While the actions used in recognition and appreciation can appear similar, the goal of appreciation is different: *to communicate and affirm the value of the individual.*

Using the analogy of plants, some plants are supposed to *produce* (like corn and apple trees) while other plants have a different purpose—

to provide shade, to give protection from the wind, or just to beautify the environment. Using recognition for those activities focused on production and applying appreciation to situations where encouragement and support is needed will bring about the best results for all involved. Working to ensure that executives, managers, HR professionals, supervisors, and employees understand that the purpose of each set of activities differs will help to facilitate using the right activities for the desired outcomes.

REFLECTION QUESTIONS

What type of employee performance issues creates the most challenges for you?

Do you think it is difficult to communicate appreciation to high-performing employees in ways not related to their performance level? Why or why not?

When you think about the solidly average employees in your organization, how does (or might) a performance-based recognition program that focuses on high achievers affect them?

What challenges come to mind when you think of trying to communicate appreciation to team members (at any level) for characteristics not directly related to their job performance?

Have you ever been complimented (or have you complimented someone else) for an action or personal characteristics not directly tied to job responsibilities? What was that experience like for you?

Do you have any difficulties seeing the differences between recognition and appreciation as they are described in this chapter? Why do you think it might be an important distinction to make?

Thinking of your work setting, give an example of when it might be best to use recognition for performance. When might it be better to show appreciation for the person himself or herself?

Have you experienced (or observed) a situation when recognition for performance was confused with appreciation at a personal level? Or when personal appreciation was communicated when recognition for performance was more appropriate? What result occurred?

CLOSING
COMMENTS

Vibrant workplaces do exist—work environments fueled by positive energy; honest interpersonal interactions laced with appreciation and encouragement; employees motivated by their personal connection to the organization's mission; workplace cultures characterized by trust, loyalty, and commitment. They are scattered across the continent and the world, and found in virtually every type of industry.

But healthy, growing workplaces don't just happen They are the result of envisioning what can be, developing a plan of how to pursue the goal, and committing resources to put the plan into action. Just wishing something will happen doesn't work.

Neither does a vibrant workplace develop quickly—at least one that will last. Actions can be taken to create the *appearance* of a positive culture. But, like weeds that grow quickly, blossom, and look good for a short time, they don't have the root system to last more than a season or endure any type of difficult circumstances, so they die and leave the space they occupied empty and barren. A thriving, supportive work environment is the result of a series of action steps, both large and small, taken over time.

As I have worked with numerous leaders and organizations, I've observed two patterns that lead nowhere:

- Attempts to *start* by implementing an all-encompassing, organization-wide plan (which never gets off the ground, dying in the mire of bureaucratic meetings); and

- Individuals (or small groups) trying to create large-scale change on their own, without eventually including important influencers within the organization.

So, what do you do? Start *somewhere*. Do *something*. Sooner is usually better than later, as is including someone else (rather than just acting totally on your own). Then as you have started your journey and you are on your way, you can meet with others to make more substantive plans.

I am excited about the wave of interest I see among leaders and everyday employees who want to learn how to make work environments healthier and more positive. And I am convinced applying the information presented here will help you achieve your goal of becoming a truly vibrant workplace. Go grow!

FREQUENTLY ASKED QUESTIONS

FAQ #1

Are there times when you shouldn't try to communicate appreciation?

Absolutely! While we know that good things happen when employees feel appreciated, communicating appreciation to staff is not a miracle salve that cures all wounds.

Sometimes, well-meaning supervisors (and, sometimes leaders who don't want to do the hard work of dealing with problems) try to use appreciation as a quick fix for deeper issues that need to be addressed. But, in fact, there are five sets of circumstances—some of them downright disturbing—when appreciation should *not* be the first action undertaken:

1. Employees are not getting paid regularly.

One time I was asked to train staff at a nonprofit organization in how to show appreciation to one another. Throughout the training, the staffers I addressed were quite passive and difficult to engage. A few days later, I found out that they had not earned regular paychecks for three months! No wonder they were disengaged!

Without honoring your agreement to pay your employees for their work, no amount of appreciation will matter.

2. Other employees have recently been laid off.

When an organization has just gone through a staff reduction, multiple issues remain. The surviving employees are processing a lot of emotions:

- Relief that they did not lose their jobs;
- Guilt that they still have a job while some of their friends do not;
- Lingering anxiety over whether there will be more layoffs or if the organization will continue to exist;
- Anger at how the layoff was handled (who was laid off and who wasn't);
- Frustrated because they believe other issues should have been dealt with (or still need to be) for the company to function well.

3. Employees are being seriously underpaid.

This can include cost-of-living adjustments, raises, or bonuses that have been put on hold. For most employees, receiving appropriate financial payment for their work is foundational to their sense of being treated fairly. While it is true that many employees tend to overvalue their own contribution and believe they should be paid more, there are clearly circumstances where it is obvious that staff is truly underpaid compared to their peers in the marketplace.

Until these issues are rectified, appreciation will feel more like a cheap substitute, since the organization is not communicating value to the employees by paying them appropriately.

4. Significant job insecurity exists.

While employees may be grateful they currently have a job, when conditions are unsettled in the overall economy, in their industry sector or in their company, they will have realistic concerns about whether they will continue to be employed in the future. Communicating appreciation to them, then, will fall on deaf ears.

Trying to say "we value you" while there are deliberations about letting people go is a blatant example of insincerity.

5. Employees have serious and valid questions about the trustworthiness of management.

There are times when management has handled situations or communication poorly, resulting in distrust. If management has been caught (or perceived to have been caught) in actions reflecting a lack of integrity (for example, handling toxic waste issues), any form of appreciation will bring skepticism and cynicism before any positive reaction can occur.

What to do?

If your organization is in the midst of these situations (or about to be), it is best to put any plan to implement any display of appreciation on hold.

Instead, *deal with the more prominent, underlying issues.* Pay your staff. Allow employees to heal after layoffs occur. Do what you can to create more job stability (and communicate with employees about it). Tell the truth. Act with integrity. Take action to rebuild trust with your employees.

Then, when the waters have calmed, reexamine whether it is indeed the right time to communicate how much you value and appreciate those who are still on your team.

FAQ #2

*Does your primary language of appreciation change over time
or in changing circumstances?*

A common (and reasonable) question asked is *"Does an individual's
preferred language of appreciation change over time?"*

From a conceptual point of view, Dr. Chapman has consistently affirmed his belief that an individual's primary *love* language in personal
relationships is highly stable over time.[1]

Similarly, it is believed people's baseline primary language of appreciation generally stays the same over time. In fact, we conducted
some research with the faculty of a private school and found that individuals' primary, secondary, and least valued languages of appreciation
were highly stable over a short period of time.

But it does appear that there can be circumstances that will influence how people desire to be shown appreciation, at least over short
periods of time. One scenario: when an employee has a highly verbal supervisor who praises them frequently, words of affirmation may become
less meaningful to them (similar to being really thirsty, drinking a lot of
water, and then wanting something else to drink). The employee may
desire appreciation communicated in different ways for a while.

Secondly, when individuals are undergoing a period of intense de-
mands and stress in their lives (either at work, or in their personal life),
Quality Time and Acts of Service often "pop up" as more desired forms
of appreciation and encouragement. This seems to be at least partially
related to culture, since in the majority North American culture, when
someone is undergoing a lot of stress, taking time to listen to them
and/or offer to help out in a practical way is a common way of demonstrating support.

What we have found, however, is that when the stressful event is
behind them, the individual's desired way of being shown appreciation
returns to the foundation of their primary language of appreciation.

The issue of the *long-term* stability of individuals' preferred languages of appreciation is still unknown. There is some anecdotal evidence that some individuals believe their preferred way of being appreciated has changed over different stages of their lives—for example, from when they were just beginning in their career to when they are more established and have supervisory responsibilities.

FAQ #3

Are there really any differences between The 5 Languages of Appreciation in the Workplace *and* The 5 Love Languages?

The foundation for *The 5 Languages of Appreciation in the Workplace*[2] and the Motivating by Appreciation Inventory[3] is based on the work done by Dr. Gary Chapman and his book *The 5 Love Languages*, which focuses on personal relationships.

While the languages discussed in both books are the same (in name), the application and expression of the languages in the work environment is often quite different than in personal relationships.

Dr. White and Dr. Chapman agreed to collaborate on exploring how the 5 languages might be applied in workplace relationships, initially focusing on identifying the parallel concept and term that would mirror the idea of "love" in personal relationships. They eventually agreed that "appreciation" seemed to be the most appropriate parallel term for communicating worth and value in the workplace.

When an individual knows their preferred love language, they shouldn't assume that their primary love language in personal relationships is the same as their most important language of appreciation in the workplace. We have found that sometimes individuals' primary languages are the same in both contexts. More often, people's primary language in one relational context (personal or work) is one of their top two languages in the other relational setting. For example, someone who has quality time as their preferred love language has a good chance of quality time being one of their top two languages of appreciation (about 65% of the time). However, depending on some of the issues we address in the book, a person's primary language can be quite different, depending on the relational context.

Additionally, there are some specific differences between *The 5 Love Languages* and *The 5 Languages of Appreciation in the Workplace* as they are applied to different types of relationships:

• **There is often a "position dynamic" associated with work-based relationships that doesn't exist in personal relationships.** A relationship between a supervisor/supervisee, employer/employee, or between two team members at different responsibility levels within the organization clearly has different relational dynamics than a personal relationship between spouses, family members, or friends.

• **Overall, a different set of expectations and boundaries exists in work-oriented relationships.** Work-based relationships usually are more formal than personal relationships. There are different social boundaries about appropriate topics of discussion, styles of communication, social settings and physical proximity than in relationships with family and friends.

• **The language of physical touch is less important in the workplace than in personal relationships**. Physical touch is the lowest language of appreciation for most people in the workplace. This makes sense—as mentioned, the workplace functions with more boundaries, and even appropriate physical touch is not desired by many in the workplace. But spontaneous, celebratory displays (high fives, fist bumps, a pat on the back) are quite common among coworkers and are an important part of positive work-based relationships.

• **Different types of quality time are valued in the workplace.** While quality time in personal relationships is primarily expressed through focused attention, other types of time are also important in work-based relationships. These may include hanging out together with colleagues, working on tasks collegially, and sharing different types of experiences to deepen team relationships.

• **When demonstrating appreciation through acts of service in the workplace, there are important conditions to meet for the act to be valued by the recipient.** Asking if the other person wants assistance, doing the service in the way the recipient wants it done, not repeatedly rescuing a colleague who is underperforming, and defining how much time you have to help—all are conditions that need to be met for the service to be viewed positively.

• **Verbal praise in front of others is used more in workplace settings.** As a love language, words of affirmation tend to be communicated more personally between two individuals. In work-based relationships, words of affirmation are often communicated in group contexts: in a team meeting, in front of customers, or at an award ceremony. Additionally, written communication through email and texting is used significantly more in work-based relationships.

• **The types of tangible gifts given differ in personal relationships and work-oriented relationships.** In personal relationships, tangible gifts tend to be things—actual objects. They are often given in celebration of a special occasion—birthday, anniversary, Christmas. And for many people, the amount spent on the gift is a significant factor. Tangible gifts in the workplace are less about the "thing" and more about the thought behind it: that the giver actually knows what is important or valued by the recipient, what hobbies or interests they have—and the gift reflects this knowledge. Also, many workplace gifts are more commonly related to experiences, such as movie tickets, gift certificates to go out to dinner, or gift cards for shopping.

Just as *The 5 Love Languages* have been found to dramatically improve marriages and friendships, so *The 5 Languages of Appreciation in the Workplace* are showing themselves to significantly improve relationships among coworkers[4] and to make workplace environments more positive for all who work there.

FAQ #4

What is the relationship between the DISC personality styles and the 5 languages of appreciation?

Numerous personality assessments are utilized in the workplace, and for a variety of reasons (screening, hiring, promotion, identifying personality type and/or communication style are a few). These assessments are quite popular and can be helpful in both understanding yourself better as well as learning how to more effectively work with your colleagues.

From the beginning of our work, we have often been asked if there is any research that illuminates the relationships that may exist between an individual's preferred language of appreciation and other personality assessments.

We are quite excited about a collaborative research project we conducted with one of the major providers and trainers of the DISC personality style inventory, with over 250 participants. We do not have the space to provide the full report here but we give a brief summary below and the complete results can be obtained at www.appreciationatwork. com/disc.

A brief introduction to the DISC

The DISC personality assessment is a tool that is widely used in the workplace to help individuals gain a better sense of themselves and others' personality style in interpersonal situations. The name "DISC" is derived from the four main personality styles it assesses: Dominance, Influence, Steadiness, and Conscientiousness. There are a number of organizations that provide both training in the use of and access to the DISC assessments. A brief description of each personality style is shown in the table on the following page.

PERSONALITY STYLE	PERSONALITY STYLE DESCRIPTION
Dominance	Person places emphasis on accomplishing results, the bottom line, confidence
Influence	Person places emphasis on influencing or persuading others, openness, relationships
Steadiness	Person places emphasis on cooperation, sincerity, dependability
Conscientiousness	Person places emphasis on quality and accuracy, expertise, competency

Research was conducted to explore the statistical relationship between the four DISC personality types and the Languages of Appreciation assessed by the *MBA Inventory*. The results of the research show that there was no correlation between the DISC personality styles and any of the Languages of Appreciation.

Practically speaking, this means that one cannot predict a person's preferred Language of Appreciation from their DISC personality type. Conversely, neither can anyone accurately predict a person's personality style from their language of appreciation.

It does appear, however, that knowing a person's DISC personality style gives another person the ability to better predict what their colleague prefers to be appreciated for. For example, a person high in the D personality style is going to want to be appreciated for *different types of actions and behaviors* (for example, taking charge in a situation) more than a person with one of the other personality styles. (This issue is explained in depth in the complete report.)[5]

Most important result

The fact that the DISC and the 5 languages of appreciation assess totally independent constructs has significant implications for leaders and organizations. Many use the DISC to help them understand a person's personality style to better communicate with them, to understand how they think about situations, their decision-making process, and what they value. This information helps their colleagues work together more effectively. On the other hand, the information provided by the *MBA Inventory* gives specific information to leaders and colleagues about how best to show appreciation, encourage, and support their team members in a way that's effective and can be perceived as authentic (versus generic and impersonal). Therefore, utilizing the 5 languages of appreciation is critical to help team members whom you have worked hard to bring together to work effectively as part of the team.

In summary, the DISC can provide valuable information for selecting and successfully incorporating new employees into their respective work group, while the *MBA Inventory* gives important information on how to keep key team members engaged and employed. When utilized together, the DISC and *MBA Inventory* provide collaborative information on *how* to effectively communicate appreciation and *for what* colleagues want to be shown appreciation.

FREE EBOOK AND ADDITIONAL RESOURCES

My goal is to provide leaders and organizations as many resources as possible to help make them successful in becoming a vibrant workplace. I have numerous other articles, videos, training materials, and resources that I have created, and I continue to create more all the time. But in a book, at some point, you have to say (and the publisher says): "Enough!" So we will end the content provided in this book here, but I want to offer you additional FREE content electronically. There are two ways to do this: first, through the eBook I have created that will give you a number of articles on a variety of topics and practical issues for applying authentic appreciation in the workplace; and second, through our website, www.appreciationatwork.com, where we give access to instructional videos, over 100 articles you can link to, and other resources you can explore (training materials, visual aids to use in the workplace, etc.). Topics include how (or whether) to communicate appreciation during Thanksgiving, Christmas, New Year's, Valentine's Day, Employee Appreciation Days, Boss's Day, and virtually every special circumstance that comes up in the workplace.

To receive your FREE eBook, *Communicating Appreciation in Special Circumstances: Holidays, Appreciation Days, and Other Awkward Situations*, email us at ebook@thevibrantworkplace.com with "Vibrant Workplace free eBook" in the subject line, and we will send you a copy (one per email address).

NOTES

Introduction

1. Stacia Sherman Garr, "The State of Employee Recognition in 2012," *SHRM Globoforce* (June 2012).
2. Rainer Strack, Carsten von der Linden, Mike Booker, and Andrea Strohmayer, "Decoding Global Talent—200,000 Survey Responses on Global Mobility and Employment Preferences," *Boston Consulting Group Survey* (October 2014).
3. "Employee Appreciation Survey," *Glassdoor* (November 2013), https://www.glassdoor.com/press/employees-stay-longer-company-bosses-showed-appreciation-glassdoor-survey/.
4. "The Year's Most Absurd Excuses for Calling- in Sick," CareerBuilder (Harris Poll, 2014), http://www.careerbuilder.com/share/aboutus/pressreleasesdetail.aspx.
5. Amy Adkins, "Majority of Employees Not Engaged Despite Gains in 2014," *Gallup* (January 2015), http://www.gallup.com/poll/181289/majority-employees-not-engaged-despite-gains-2014.aspx.
6. Teresa A. Daniel and Gary S. Metcalf, "The Fundamentals of Employee Recognition," *SHRM White Paper* (May 2005).

Chapter 1: Your Leaders Aren't Interested

1. Teresa A. Daniel and Gary S. Metcalf, "The Fundamentals of Employee Recognition," *SHRM White Paper* (May 2005).
2. T. A. Judge, R. F. Piccolo, N. P. Podsakoff, J. C. Shaw, and B. L. Rich, "The Relationship between Pay and Job Satisfaction: A Meta-Analysis of the Literature," *Journal of Vocational Behavior* 77, no. 2 (2010): 157–67.
3. Edward L. Deci, Richard Koestner, and Richard M. Ryan, "A meta-analytic review of experiments examining the effects of extrinsic rewards on intrinsic motivation," *Psychological Bulletin* 125, no. 6 (November 1999): 627–68, http://dx.doi.org/10.1037/0033-2909.125.6.627.
4. Yoon Jik Cho and James Perry, "Intrinsic Motivation and Employee Attitudes: Role of Managerial Trustworthiness, Goal Directedness, and Extrinsic Reward Expectancy," *Review of Public Administration* (November 2011). doi:10.1177/0734371X11421495.
5. Thomas Chamarro-Premuzic, "Does Money Really Affect Motivation? A Review of the Literature," *Harvard Business Review,* http://hbr.org/2013/04/does-money-really-affect-motiv.
6. Martin Dewhurst, Matthew Guthridge, and Elizabeth Mohr, "Motivating People: Getting Beyond Money," *McKinsey Quarterly* (November 2009).
7. Sami Abbasi and Moncef Belhadjali, "A Closer Look at Millennials at Work: A Literature Review," *International Journal of Humanities and Social Science Review* 2, no. 4 (June 2016).

8. Rick Maurer, *Beyond the Wall of Resistance* (Austin, TX: Bard Press, 2010).
9. See www.appreciationatwork.com/aawrs.

Chapter 2: Two Big Questions Supervisors Ask

1. Rex Huppke, "Chicago's Top Workplaces," *Chicago Tribune* (November 2013).
2. Rainer Strack et al, "Decoding Global Talent—200,000 Survey Response on Global Mobility and Employment Preferences," *Boston Consulting Group Survey* (October 2014).
3. Leigh Branham, *The 7 Hidden Reasons Employees Leave: How to Recognize the Subtle Signs and Act Before It's Too Late* (New York: AMACOM, 2005), 24.
4. R. A. Emmons and Michael McCullough, "Counting Blessings Versus Burdens: An Experimental Investigation of Gratitude and Subjective Well-Being in Daily Life," *Journal of Personality and Social Psychology* 11, no. 1 (February 2003): 52–60.
5. Roland Zahn, Jorge Moll, Mirella Paiva, Griselda Garrido, Frank Krueger, Edward Huey, Jordan Grafman, "The Neural Basis of Human Social Values: Evidence from Functional MRI," *Cerebral Cortex* 19, no. 2 (Feb. 2009): 276–83.
6. Alex Korb, "The Grateful Brain," *Psychology Today* (November 2012), https://www.psychologytoday.com/blog/prefrontal-nudity/201211/the-grateful-brain.

Chapter 3: Why Recognition Programs Don't Work

1. Teresa A. Daniel and Gary S. Metcalf, "The Fundamentals of Employee Recognition," *SHRM White Paper* (May 2005).
2. Amy Adkins, "Employee Engagement in U.S. Stagnant in 2015," *Gallup* (January 2016), http://www.gallup.com/poll/188144/employee-engagement-stagnant-2015.aspx.
3. Jim Collins, *Good to Great* (New York: Harper Business, 2001).

Chapter 4: Negativity

1. Kimberly Schaufenbuel, "Motivation on the Brain – Applying the Neuroscience of Motivation in the Workplace," *UNC Kenan Flagler Business School*, 2015.
2. Michael Miller, ed., "In Praise of Gratitude," *Harvard Mental Health Letter* 28, no. 5 (November 2011).
3. Jennifer Robison, "In Praise of Praising Your Employees," *Business Journal* (November 2006), http://www.gallup.com/businessjournal/25369/praise-praising-your-employees.aspx.

Chapter 5: Busyness

1. Go to www.mbainventory.com for more information.
2. Leigh Branham, *The 7 Hidden Reasons Employees Leave: How to Recognize the Subtle Signs and Act Before It's Too Late* (New York: AMACOM, 2005), 24.

Chapter 7: People Are Different—But We Treat Them the Same

1. Daniel Goleman. "Three Kinds of Empathy: Cognitive, Emotional, Compassionate" (June 2007), www.danielgoleman.info/three-kinds-of-empathy-cognitive-emotional-compassionate/.

Chapter 8: Can Appreciation Cross Cultures?

1. Erin Meyer, *Culture Map: Breaking Through the Invisible Boundaries of Global Business* (New York: Public Affairs, 2014).

Chapter 9: Colleagues Who Are Hard to Appreciate

1. Paul White, Gary Chapman, and Harold Myra, *Rising Above a Toxic Workplace: Taking Care of Yourself in an Unhealthy Environment* (Chicago: Northfield, 2014).

Chapter 10: Performance Issues: Underachievers, Overachievers, and Everything in Between

1. Thomas Chamarro-Premuzic, "Does Money Really Affect Motivation? A Review of the Literature," *Harvard Business Review,* http://hbr.org/2013/04/does-money-really-affect-motiv.

2. Martin Dewhurst, Matthew Guthridge, and Elizabeth Mohr, "Motivating People: Getting Beyond Money," *McKinsey Quarterly* (November 2009).

FAQs

1. Gary Chapman, *The 5 Love Languages: The Secret to Love That Lasts* (Chicago: Northfield, 2004).

2. Gary Chapman and Paul White, *The 5 Languages of Appreciation in the Workplace* (Chicago: Northfield, 2011).

3. Paul White, the *Motivating by Appreciation Inventory,* www.mbainventory.com.

4. Paul White, "*Appreciation at Work* training and the *Motivating by Appreciation Inventory*: development and validity," *Strategic HR Review* 15, no. 1 (January 2016).

5. Paul White, "The Relationship between the DISC Personality Assessment and the 5 Languages of Appreciation," *Training* (November 2016).

ACKNOWLEDGMENTS

I am thankful that I don't have to complete tasks on my own. If I did, they would not get done, be finished on time, and the quality would be much lower! Many people helped in a variety of ways to assist in getting *The Vibrant Workplace* completed.

First and foremost, my wife, Kathy, has been the steady force on which I could depend—dialoguing about ideas, proofreading initial drafts, encouraging me, and doing all of those little things that allowed me to focus my time and energy on writing. Without her, this book would have never happened.

My team at Appreciation at Work also were invaluable in giving me input and feedback on ideas, wording, and how the content hit them (especially my millennials!), as well as practical, logistical help on a daily basis. Thanks to: Debi Abood, Nevi Castro-Miller, Erin Ellsworth, Tim Hepner, Seth Michelson, Michele Thiessen, and Becky Rogers. And a special note of thanks in memory of Barbara Bath, a delightful, joyful team member whom we lost suddenly in the midst of the project.

To all who shared their stories and gave valuable insights regarding the specific work settings in which they serve, I am grateful for the practical suggestions you provided. I know others in your fields will be encouraged by your input. Thanks to: Dan Agne, Brian Henry, Katy Henry, Michelle Hepner, Kathy Schoonover-Shoffner, Richard Shoffner, Caroline White, Nathan White, Terry Williams, and Kim Yearyean.

Additionally, I received valuable insights from our partners who are sharing authentic appreciation with organizations internationally.

I find this aspect of our work to be fascinating, challenging, and encouraging—all simultaneously. Thank you for the work you are doing and allowing me to learn alongside you: Rengin Akkemik, Paul Choi, Anita Fevang, Sofie Halkjær, Jasmine Liew, Pat McGrath, Caroline Rochon, Roy Saunderson, Liselotte Søndergaard, and John Sung.

Finally, I'm grateful to the professional support I've received over the years from Dr. Chapman and from the team at Northfield Publishing. Without Gary's trust, support, mentoring, and encouragement, none of our work to improve workplace relationships would have ever happened. To John Hinkley, Betsey Newenhuyse, Zack Williamson, and the rest of the staff at Northfield, you have provided the channels for me to impact hundreds of thousands of employees, managers, and workplaces. I am deeply appreciative!

ABOUT THE AUTHOR

Paul White, PhD, is a psychologist, speaker, consultant, and coauthor of three books, including the bestselling *The 5 Languages of Appreciation in the Workplace*. Dr. White specializes in assisting businesses, organizations and governmental agencies in developing positive workplace cultures, building healthy relationships, and avoiding negative patterns that lead to toxicity. Frequently published in top leadership, business, and human resources publications and cited by major media sources, Dr. White has spoken to conferences and organizations on four continents. He has significantly improved the daily work lives within Fortune 100 companies, medical and long-term care facilities, governmental agencies, colleges and universities, public and private schools, financial institutions, ministries and nonprofit organizations, and manufacturing firms in more than twenty countries. Dr. White brings challenging, yet practical information to his audiences and readers in a down-to-earth and humorous manner. He also is an amateur arborist and wannabe tournament fisherman.

TO CONTACT PAUL WHITE:

Paul White, PhD
Appreciation at Work
111 S. Whittier, Suite 3000
Wichita, KS 67228
316-681-4431
admin@drpaulwhite.com

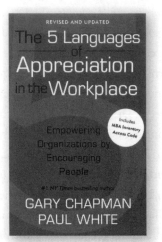
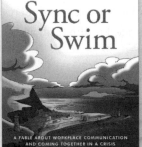